ORTHO

ALL ABOUT POWER TOOLS

Meredith® Books
Des Moines, Iowa

Ortho® Books
An imprint of Meredith® Books

All About Power Tool Basics
Editor: Larry Johnston
Contributing Writer: Martin Miller
Senior Associate Design Director: Tom Wegner
Assistant Editor: Harijs Priekulis
Copy Chief: Terri Fredrickson
Copy and Production Editor: Victoria Forlini
Editorial Operations Manager: Karen Schirm
Managers, Book Production: Pam Kvitne,
    Marjorie J. Schenkelberg
Contributing Copy Editor: James Stepp
Technical Proofreader: George Granseth
Contributing Proofreaders: Kathy Roth Eastman,
    Ray Kast, Steve Salato
Indexer: Barbara L. Klein
Electronic Production Coordinator: Paula Forest
Editorial and Design Assistant: Renee E. McAtee,
    Karen McFadden

Additional Editorial Contributions from
    Art Rep Services
Director: Chip Nadeau
Designers: lk Design
Illustrator: Dave Brandon

Meredith® Books
Publisher and Editor in Chief: James D. Blume
Design Director: Matt Strelecki
Managing Editor: Gregory H. Kayko
Executive Editor, Gardening and Home Improvement:
    Benjamin W. Allen
Executive Editor, Home Improvement: Larry Erickson

Director, Operations: George A. Susral
Director, Production: Douglas M. Johnston

Vice President and General Manager: Douglas J. Guendel

Meredith Publishing Group
President, Publishing Group: Stephen M. Lacy
Vice President-Publishing Director: Bob Mate

Meredith Corporation
Chairman and Chief Executive Officer: William T. Kerr
Chairman of the Executive Committee: E.T. Meredith III

Photographers
    (Photographers credited may retain copyright ©
    to the listed photographs.)
L = Left, R = Right, C = Center, B = Bottom, T = Top
Arrow Fastener Co., Inc.: 49T
King Au/Studio Au: 9TC, 58, 67T
Baldwin Photography: 6, 35TR and inset, 36T, 37B, 42B,
    48TL, 68TR, 79T, 80
DeWalt: 11TL, 19, 27, 29BC, 34, 50BR, 78B
Dremel: 46C, 47TL, 48 TCL, BCL, TC, TR, B, 70TL
Freud, Inc.: 24B, 37T, 38BR
Grizzly Industrial, Inc.: 67B, 72TL, 78T, 79B, 82, 83CR
John Hetherington: 4TL, 14B, 29TC, 33B, 35CR, BL,
    38BL, 41, 47TR, 51T, B, 52T, 54BL, 66TR, 68BL, 76B,
    86TL, TR, 93TL, TC, TR, CR
Hetherington Photography: 10, 11TR, 24T, 42B, 73T
Hitachi Power Tools: 7, 63
William Hopkins Sr.: 5, 50TL, 68TL, 72TR, 76TR
Wm. Hopkins: 4BL, 9TR, 30, 40TL, TR, 42TR, 74, 87B
InsideOut Studio: 20, 21, 26, 29T, 31, 35BR, 38T, C, 50TR,
    54, 55, 59, 64, 68BR, 73B, 83TL,TR, 92BL, BR, 93B
Jet Equipment and Tools, Inc.: 40B, 52B, 53B, 76TL, 83BR,
    86B
Jim Kascoutas: 18, 70B
Makita U.S.A., Inc.: 13TR, 29B, 32, 33T, 33C, 36B, 42TL,
    62, 63
Ryobi Technologies: 4BR, 12, 53T, 92TL
Greg Scheidemann: 46T, 47B
Shopsmith, Inc.: 90TR, CL, 91TR
Smithy Co.: 90TL, 91TL, BR
Dean Tanner/Primary Image: 50BL, 70TR
Steve Uzzell: 8
Steve Whelan/Laguna Tools: 90BL, 91TC
Zane Williams: 44, 49B, 66TL
On the cover: Hetherington Photography

All of us at Ortho® Books are dedicated to providing you
with the information and ideas you need to enhance your
home and garden. We welcome your comments and
suggestions about this book. Write to us at:
    Meredith Corporation
    Ortho Books
    1716 Locust St.
    Des Moines, IA 50309–3023

If you would like to purchase any of our home improvement,
gardening, cooking, crafts, or home decorating and design
books, check wherever quality books are sold. Or visit us at:
meredithbooks.com

If you would like more information on other Ortho
products, call 800-225-2883 or visit us at: www.ortho.com

POWER TOOLS FOR THE HOMEOWNER 4

PORTABLE POWER TOOLS 10

STATIONARY AND BENCHTOP TOOLS 50

POWER TOOLS FOR THE HOMEOWNER

Whether you're hanging a picture or remodeling a room, power tools can make the job faster, easier, and often safer. Power tools let you tackle otherwise difficult or time-consuming jobs with ease. Fastening a mailbox to your brick house, for instance, becomes relatively easy when you can drill holes for anchors with a masonry bit and portable electric drill—or even better, a hammer drill. The same chore with a star drill and hammer is slow, tedious work. A power tool often helps you do a job better. Consider cutting a number of boards to length for shelving. Making a square cut calls for care and skill with a handsaw. A portable

Power tools make home maintenance, remodeling, and woodworking projects easier, faster, and frequently safer. They often allow you to do jobs more accurately than you could with hand tools.

circular saw makes square cuts quickly and accurately.

Once considered the domain of professionals and serious hobbyists, power tools now are designed and priced for the casual do-it-yourselfer. What's more, cordless tools offer true portability—you can work anywhere in the house or yard (or even in the deep woods if you wish) without having to be within a cord's reach of an electrical outlet.

Many of today's medium-price tools boast features, power, and durability that once could be found only in high-price, professional-grade tools. And in today's market, finding the right tool at the right price is not a problem. Home centers and hardware stores sell portable power tools, such as drills, sanders, and circular saws, along with stationary tools, such as table saws and drill presses, in a wide range of prices. You also can buy power tools from catalog outlets, lumberyards, and general merchandise retailers—even over the Internet.

There's a wealth of information about both portable and stationary power tools in this book. You'll learn how each tool fits the needs of your toolbox or workshop. The pages devoted to each tool describe its features and functions and tell about accessories that can increase versatility. Basic information on how to use the tool is included, along with tips that make completing jobs quicker or easier. In addition, the book covers basic material for setting up and maintaining stationary tools.

SAFETY

Modern tools are so easy to use and have so many safety features that it's easy to forget they pose potential hazards. Saws, lathes, routers, and other tools throw sharp chips into the air with tremendous speed. Blades cut quickly. Motors scream. Even a seemingly innocuous palm sander can spew dust hazardous to breathing.

Here's a basic safety checklist that will keep your use of power tools safe and enjoyable.

■ Protect your eyes with industrial-quality safety glasses —the ones with side shields. Look for a "Z87.1" label on the glasses or goggles—that tells you they're industrial strength. Get prescription safety glasses if you need them. Wear a full face shield for the most complete protection against flying material.

■ Long-term exposure to power-tool noise can harm your hearing. Ear protection comes in various styles, from foam ear plugs and pads to noise-activated earmuffs that raise the level of protection as noise increases. You can even get

combination earmuffs and safety goggles. Find protection that's comfortable—if it doesn't feel right, you're likely not to wear it.

■ Wear proper clothing—gloves for rough work, wrist and back supports, and knee pads. Avoid loose, baggy clothing that can get caught in machinery. Clothing that's so tight it restricts your movement can be dangerous too. Tuck long hair under a cap; even if your hair is short, wear a cap to keep debris out of it. Boots are a wise choice for any task that requires power tools. At a minimum, wear rubber-soled shoes to minimize slipping. When the tool kicks up a lot of dust, wear a tight-fitting mask or respirator.

■ Schedule your time so you can keep your mind on your work. Keep the work area clean and your tools clean, sharp, and in good repair. Don't remove tool guards for any reason. Always know the location of the power switch, and unplug all tools before servicing them.

TOOL BUYING TIPS

The tests and ratings of power tools found in woodworking magazines are valuable sources of information when you're shopping for tools. This benchtop planer is being tested by WOOD magazine to determine its current draw and cutter speed under load.

Tool buying has changed a lot since power tools came on the market more than 60 years ago. Like all change, there are advantages and drawbacks.

On one hand, today's power-tool market is a do-it-yourselfer's paradise—there is a tool for almost every task and budget. On the other, the sheer volume of models, styles, and accessories—and the fact that one job can often be done by more than one tool—can leave the prospective buyer overwhelmed with choices.

The best way to start shopping for power tools is to inventory the kind of work you plan to do with them.

INVENTORY YOUR NEEDS

Before you head to the nearest home center or tool outlet, list the work you intend to accomplish in the near future. Start with the project that got you thinking about buying a tool in the first place. Perhaps you need only tools that will make routine maintenance tasks go more quickly. Perhaps you've decided to finally build your dream deck. Maybe it's time to remodel the basement or attic to add more room to your home.

Once you've jotted down your immediate needs, list the tools needed for those jobs.

Routine maintenance may require only a power drill or drill/driver and a few basic hand tools. Deck building will likely call for a cordless drill/driver and a circular saw. For large-scale remodeling, you may want to add a table saw or miter saw. Craft work and woodworking projects like furniture making will add to your list. You may need a jigsaw, router, drill press, band saw, planer, and jointer—and enough space for them.

As you make your list, remember that many jobs can be done by more than one tool. A portable drill will drill holes, and so will a drill press. Driving 300 decking screws will go quickly with a portable drill, but if you're building bookcases with adjustable shelves you'll need a drill press to space holes evenly.

You can cut miters and bevels with a circular saw, but also with a radial arm saw, table saw, or miter saw. A circular saw is the one to use for miter-cutting deck boards at a corner; one of the others would be a better choice for making picture frames with perfect corners. A belt sander will sand wood surfaces smooth, but so will a random-orbit palm sander. You may need both if you're turning rough stock into a tabletop.

What you buy depends on how you will use the tool. What you gain as you move from portable to stationary tools (and as costs increase) is accuracy, flexibility, and consistent high-quality results. What you lose is portability. The sections in this book that list the functions of each tool will help you decide what tool is right for your job.

PRO-QUALITY TOOLS

Professional-quality tools are made from higher quality components than tools designed for occasional use—ball or needle bearings instead of bushings, precisely machined gears instead of die-cast or nonmetallic gears, one piece housings, switches with dust boots, and hatches that allow you to change worn-out brushes. Some of these differences are apparent from the outside; others won't show unless you take the tool apart.

A homeowner-grade tool, however, might be a smart buy if you will use it infrequently for jobs in which continued accuracy isn't a requirement. The best rule to follow for tool purchases is this: Buy the highest-quality tool you can afford.

HOW OFTEN WILL YOU USE IT?

While you're pondering your prospective purchases, consider how often you will use the tool. Infrequent use means inexpensive, homeowner-grade equipment could suit your needs. Frequent use will demand heavy-duty tools that cost more.

When considering how much you'll use a tool, remember this: Once you've bought a particular power tool, you'll find additional uses for it, and you may find yourself taking on more projects.

MATCH YOUR SKILLS

Plan ahead so your tool purchases match the development of your skills. As your skills improve, your tool inventory will grow. If you decide that most of your immediate work will require only a circular saw, make that your first purchase. Then look for a lumberyard or woodworking shop that will do occasional jointing, planing, and other jobs you aren't equipped to do for a moderate fee.

SMART SHOPPING

When shopping, visit several stores, read all the catalogs you can find, check out the Internet outlets (there's a list of manufacturers' websites at the end of this book), read tool reviews in woodworking magazines, and look for sales and specials. The list price of a tool won't tell you much—almost all tools are available for less than list.

Don't rush your purchases. Familiarize yourself with the features of different models and avoid overkill—if a 1-hp router will meet your needs, don't buy a 3-hp unit. Take the tool off the rack to get a sense for how it feels in your hand. Test its weight and balance.

Once you've settled on a particular model, search for the best price. Expensive equipment like lathes and other stationary tools may cost hundreds of dollars less from one competitor to the next. When making Internet or catalog purchases, include shipping costs in your price comparisons; the price, including shipping, might be the same as, or even more than, the same tool just down the street at your local home center—and you won't have to wait for it. Also consider whether service and advice from a local dealer would be available from mail-order sources.

CORDLESS TOOLS

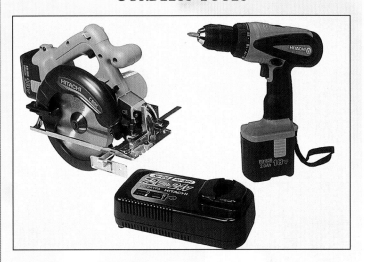

Cordless tools have revolutionized the market. The most popular is the cordless drill/driver, but you'll also find cordless reciprocating saws, circular saws, jigsaws—even chain saws and miter saws.

Although cordless tools bring increased portability and convenience to a project, they have some disadvantages:
■ They usually cost more than corded versions.
■ Use and run time depend on the battery charge and capacity. The tool must be kept charged to be ready for use. (Whenever possible, buy two batteries; you can use one while the other is recharging.)
■ Worn-out batteries may be expensive to replace.

Cordless-tool batteries range from 7.2 to 24 volts. Drills come in all voltages; other tools come with the high-voltage battery packs.

You'll find nickel-cadmium (Nicad) batteries in most tools you shop for, but nickel metal hydride (NiMH) batteries are moving into the market. They provide more run time with less weight.

SETTING UP SHOP

Large or small, workshops require careful planning and layout so work flows smoothly from one tool to the next. The layout of this shop demonstrates how even a medium-size room can accommodate all the tools required for almost any woodworking project.

Working in a well-organized workshop is efficient and pleasurable. But in a disorganized shop even simple projects can become chores that leave you feeling frustrated and worn out.

This is true for shops of all sizes. Large shops can be easier to organize, but even in small spaces, you can beat the squeeze with a little planning.

ORGANIZING THE WORKFLOW

The key to well-planned shop space is creating a smooth flow between the stages of a project. Most projects generally proceed in the following order:

■ **RAW MATERIAL INTAKE AND STORAGE** Make entrances and storage spaces large enough for lumber and sheet goods.

■ **CUTTING STOCK TO SIZE** Place tools for crosscutting, resawing, ripping, jointing, and planing near the intake and storage area.

■ **ASSEMBLY** Allow space for completing parts and assembling them. Place tools for these tasks near your workbench.

■ **FINISHING** Provide a well-ventilated, dust-free place for applying stains, paints, and varnishes.

WORKFLOW PATTERNS

The size and shape of your shop will determine how the steps above fit your floor plan. Some shops lend themselves to an in-line layout. Long, narrow shops might call for a U-shape workflow. Rectangular shops often suit themselves to circular layouts. There is no one ideal pattern. The way your shop takes shape will depend on its configuration and the tools you plan to use. Save yourself some time by making layout decisions on paper before moving tools.

TYPICAL LAYOUT OF LONG, NARROW SHOP SPACE

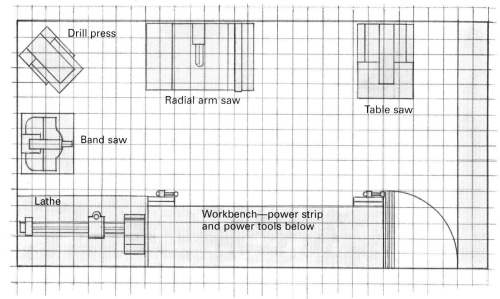

Drill press

Radial arm saw

Table saw

Band saw

Lathe

Workbench—power strip and power tools below

IMPROVING THE SHOP ENVIRONMENT

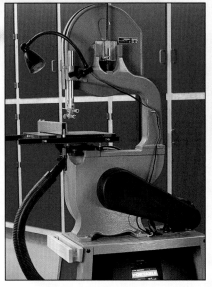

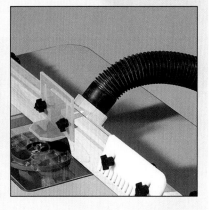

Tool arrangement is only one aspect of making your shop a comfortable place to work. To get the most enjoyment out of your shop, make it warm in the winter, cool in the summer, well-lit, and as dust-free as possible.

In cold climates, insulate both the walls and ceilings with fiberglass batts or blankets; finish the surfaces with drywall. Install a heater if necessary. An electric heater is safer than gas (it won't ignite fumes from finishes as readily), but slightly more expensive. Add a dehumidifier in damp climates or basements.

Make sure you plan enough general and task lighting. Position tools near windows if possible and use overhead four-tube fluorescent fixtures with 4-foot, 80-watt bulbs. You can check your general lighting by putting a wood block at various workstations around the room. The block shouldn't cast shadows.

Add task lighting to each workstation, especially over workbenches and on stationary tools. You can modify small flexible-arm lamps and attach them to a tool housing, or you can use task lights on portable stands.

Controlling dust is a must. Breathing the remnants of your work is not healthy, and dust on tools interferes with your sight and their operation. Dusty floors pose a safety hazard. At a minimum, connect a shop vacuum to the dust-collection port on the tool you're using. If your budget allows, invest in a single-stage or two-stage dust-collection system. An overhead air cleaner can keep the air dust-free.

PAPER PLANS AND TRIANGLES

Draw the shop to scale on graph paper with a ¼-inch grid. Label the areas for intake, rough cutting, assembly, and finishing.

Cut out paper templates of your tools, also to scale, and position them on your plan, leaving 18- to 24-inch walkways between stationary tools. Leave enough room at the infeed and outfeed sides for long stock.

Start your arrangement with your workbench template. The workbench (at least 4 feet long and 24 inches deep) is the hub of your shop. If you're cramped for space, be creative. Make the workbench the same height as your table saw so it can double as an outfeed support when you cut large stock. Extend your table saw with a laminate-covered router table. If you don't have room for a table saw, put a radial arm saw along a wall. Stand the drill press in a corner.

Try to arrange the tools in each area in compact triangles so you won't have to walk long distances as you work within each area.

Once you're satisfied with the arrangement, use tracing paper to draw in your wiring and lighting plans.

ROLLING THE STOCK

In a small shop, you may be tempted to put your stationary tools on wheels and move them out of the way when they're not needed. Instead, equip your shop with a rolling cart or two and move subassemblies and hand tools from station to station. It may be easier to move the project than it is to move large tools. Moving a tool may jar it out of alignment. If your shop layout demands some movable tools, use sturdy, well-engineered mobile bases with locking casters or retractable legs.

PORTABLE POWER TOOLS

Modern tool design and manufacturing technology have revolutionized power tools. Plus, you don't even have to be near an electrical outlet to use many of today's power tools. Lightweight high-tech plastic housings, more powerful lightweight motors, enhanced safety features, and greater manufacturing precision have made them easier and safer to use, while cutting their once prohibitive prices and expanding the number of models available.

For almost every task there is a portable power tool that can help. And you can find one to fit your budget—it's often more economical to buy a tool than to rent one. Constantly changing technology brings ever-better tools; cordless drills now run longer and work harder than just a few years ago, for example. Now cordless circular saws and other tools share the drill's battery.

The number of available features and range of prices make buying a power tool a complex job. This chapter will take some of the confusion out of that process. Here, you'll find information to help you make decisions about what tool you need and how to find the one that lets you stay within your budget.

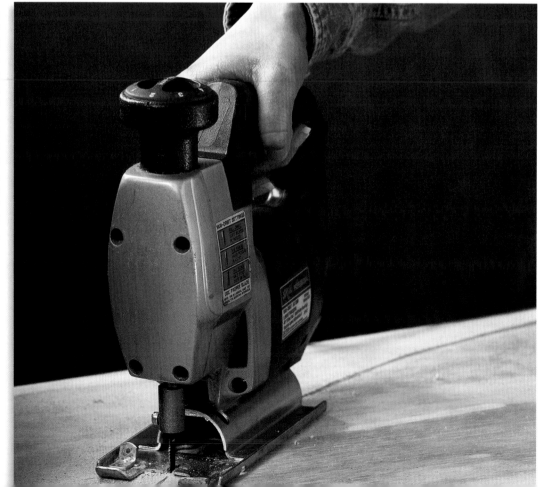

There's a portable power tool for almost every task, from drilling holes to cutting sweeping curves in plywood. With power at your fingertips and modern ergonomics, today's tools fit every woodworker and every budget.

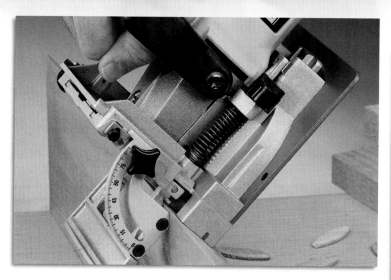

EXTENSION CORDS

Using corded power tools often requires an extension cord. Before you plug in the tool, make sure your extension cord is up to the job. Damaged insulation on a cord can shock you. A cord that's too long or one with damaged or undersized conductors restricts current flow, causing the cord to overheat. This can trip the circuit breaker, damage the tool, or even start a fire.

Extension cords carry ratings for their use—either indoor or outdoor, or both—but your decision about which to use should not stop there. Consider also the length of the cord and its wire size. Wire sizes are designated by gauge numbers; smaller numbers indicate larger conductor diameter and, thus, larger current capacity. Before you start to work, check the amperage of the tool on its faceplate. Then calculate the distance between the outlet and the work site. Refer to the chart below to make sure the wire size will handle the load for the length of cord you need. You can use a heavier-gauge wire (a smaller number) than the one listed, but not a lighter gauge.

Heavy, well-insulated cords are a wise investment. Always use three-pronged cords and grounded receptacles. When working outdoors, plug the cord into a ground-fault circuit interrupter (GFCI). Uncoil the cord so it doesn't develop kinks, which can damage the conductors. Protect the cord from sharp edges, and if it crosses a walkway, tape it down with duct tape.

MAXIMUM LENGTH AND WIRE SIZE FOR EXTENSION CORDS

		Cord Length				
	25'	50'	75'	100'	150'	200'
Tool Amperage*			Wire Size			
0–2.0	18	18	18	18	16	16
2.1–3.4	18	18	18	16	14	14
3.5–5.0	18	18	16	14	12	12
5.1–7.0	18	16	14	12	10	10
7.1–12.0	16	14	12	10	8	8
12.1–16.0	14	12	10	8	8	6

For 115-volt tools at full load, amperage as listed on tool specification plate. Check instruction manual for limitations specific to the tool.

GENERAL CARE

Power tools are designed for rugged work, and a few simple maintenance practices will extend their usefulness and keep them out of the repair shop.

■ Help your tools keep cool by blowing out dust from the ventilation openings with an air compressor or shop vacuum. (Be sure to wear eye protection.)

■ Keep blades and bits sharp and change abrasives when they're worn out. Dull cutting surfaces and abrasives make the tool work harder and generate heat.

■ Don't force a tool through the work. That overloads the motor and can cause blades and bits to bend or wear prematurely.

■ Lubricate drill chucks and tool adjustment points with lubricants containing PTFE, but keep lubricants out of the motor and gears. Most modern tools don't need additional lubrication, and excess lubricant can cause dirt buildup.

■ Check motor brushes periodically and change them when they're worn. Excessive heat and sparking are signs your brushes need attention.

DRILL/DRIVER

The portable electric drill can help with so many tasks that it ranks as everyone's basic power tool. It's a good tool to buy first. When you buy a drill, spend a little extra for a high-quality model: It will last a long time and will probably be one of your most-used tools.

BUYING AN ELECTRIC DRILL

Corded or cordless? That's the first decision you face when buying an electric drill. Either type, with proper bits and accessories, will drill holes, drive or remove screws, sand, grind, file, rasp, buff, and perform a variety of other chores.

A DRILL/DRIVER CAN...

■ Drill holes
■ Drive and remove screws
■ Cut mortises
■ Sand, saw, grind, rasp, shine, and cut plugs (with accessories and stands)

Cordless drills, popular and convenient to use, are classified by battery voltage. A drill with a 9.6- or 12-volt battery is well-suited to household use. Higher-voltage models provide more power and longer run time, but they are heavier and more expensive.

Most cordless drills are marketed as drill/drivers, which means they have a

HAMMER DRILLS

If any of your future do-it-yourself projects call for drilling into masonry, tile, or concrete, include a hammer drill on your shopping list. You may be planning to tile your bath, attach a deck to the foundation wall, install new electric outlets in the basement, or attach a handrail to the concrete steps. These are projects waiting for a hammer drill.

A hammer drill combines the rotary action of a drill with the percussive action of a hammer. A hammer drill equipped with a proper bit can drill a $^3/_8$-inch hole 2 inches deep in large-aggregate concrete in about 30 seconds. With a standard drill and masonry bit, the same hole would take you about five minutes.

Hammer drills for home use come with $^3/_8$- or $^1/_2$-inch chucks—the $^3/_8$-inch model should be able to take care of most of your projects. You can rent one if your masonry work will be infrequent, but the drill can double as a standard wood-drilling tool with the flick of a switch.

Percussion bits are made to take the pounding action dished out by a hammer drill—regular masonry bits are not. The hammering action will quickly blunt the tip of a regular masonry bit.

When you use the tool, screw the auxiliary handle into the side of the drill to steady it. After you tighten the bit and adjust the depth-stop rod (most hammer drills come with one), place the drill tip on the work and start the drill. Don't force the drill; use only enough pressure to guide it. Let the tool do the work.

clutch that can be locked for drilling or adjusted to disengage at a preset torque so you don't drive the screws too deep. This useful feature is worth the cost, but you probably won't need more than 5–10 clutch settings.

After you've bought your first cordless drill, you may wonder how you ever got along without one. Like other cordless tools, however, they have some drawbacks: They cost more initially, you must keep the battery charged between uses (or have two for continuous drilling), and replacing a worn-out battery is costly.

With a corded drill, you don't have to wait for the battery to charge, and the tool will run as long as you keep the electric bill paid. The drill is always ready to use. A corded drill usually weighs less than a cordless model of similar power—an advantage when you're working off a ladder or over your head.

Corded drills, too, have some disadvantages: You almost always need to drag out an extension cord—sometimes a long one—and working outdoors or in a damp area could be hazardous. Most don't have a clutch for screwdriving.

Clutch to set screwdriving torque

Speed-range selector

Chuck

Variable-speed trigger

Forward/reverse switch

Centered handle

Battery pack

WHAT SIZE DRILL?

After you decide whether a corded or cordless model will fit your needs, size is the next decision. Drill size is commonly designated by the largest shank that will fit into the chuck. The chuck of a ⅜-inch drill will hold a ⅜-inch shank, but that doesn't mean that's the largest hole you can drill with it. Twist drills and bits to bore larger holes are made with shanks that will fit a ⅜-inch drill.

A ⅜-inch model is ideal for most household tasks. A ½-inch drill usually boasts more power in addition to the increased chuck capacity, but it is larger and heavier, too. On the other hand, a light-duty ¼-inch drill might prove disappointing on some tasks.

KEYED AND KEYLESS CHUCKS

If you're buying a ⅜-inch corded drill, consider one with a keyless chuck. Instead of tightening the jaws of the chuck with a key, you tighten it by twisting the nose with your hand. They're common on cordless models and not available on ½-inch corded drills. Although some argue that keyless chucks are hard to tighten enough to keep the bit from slipping, they make changing bits quick and easy. As an alternative, use a quick-change adapter in your keyed chuck.

VARIABLE SPEEDS

For maximum versatility, buy a variable-speed reversible (VSR) drill, available either corded or cordless. The variable-speed feature allows you to increase the drill speed with increased pressure on the trigger. You can start drilling slowly and use the higher speed for finishing the work. The reversible feature changes the rotation of the motor so you can withdraw screws and stuck bits.

Many cordless drills offer a transmission with two speed ranges at little extra cost. The lower range produces the higher torque necessary for driving screws, and the higher range is best for drilling. Look for ranges of about 0–400 rpm and 0–1,500 rpm for the best all-around performance.

Whichever style you buy, make sure the trigger lock is easy to click on and off and not placed where you'll engage it accidentally. A hook or a lanyard on the drill case that will hold the tool on your tool belt is handy when you're working on a ladder.

THE ELECTRIC SCREWDRIVER

Smaller and lighter than a full-size drill, but with plenty of torque for its size, the electric screwdriver is a handy tool both in the shop and around the house. It's perfect for light assembly work, especially for long, fine-thread screws such as those that attach electrical fixtures to boxes. It usually won't drive screws into wood without a pilot hole. In a pinch, some models will drill small holes too, although the slow speed is not ideal for drilling.

Cordless screwdrivers come with different types of chucks or bit holders; the ones that accept standard hexagonal-shank screwdriver bits allow you to interchange tips for slotted, phillips, and other screwdrivers. You'll find some equipped with a clutch that slips when the screw is all the way in. It's a handy feature, but not essential for most uses. They're reversible, so you can use them to extract screws, too.

Handle styles vary from model to model. Some screwdrivers are designed to snap into a wall-mounted battery charger, keeping the tool out of the way when it's not in use but ready to go when you need it.

DRILL/DRIVER
continued

A commercial drill guide makes accurate drilling easier. It can center a hole, as shown here, and keeps the bit perpendicular to the surface.

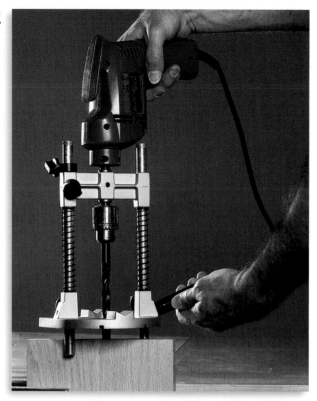

HANDLES

Cordless drills come with two handle styles—centered or pistol grip. A pistol grip lets you push directly in line with the axis of the chuck. A centered handle offers better balance. If you're in the market for a ½-inch drill, get one with a removable side handle. Heavy-duty drills, ½ inch and larger, often have a D-handle on the back.

A portable drill with a drum sander smooths both inside and outside curves.

COST

Prices for corded drills range from about $30 to more than $200; a corded drill in the $50 to $100 range will give you years of service.

Cordless drills start at about $80 and increase to more than $300 for more powerful high-voltage models. You can buy a high-quality 12-volt drill with charger and extra battery for about $130. For $20 to $30 more, you can get a 14.4-volt model.

DRILL BITS

Bits make the drill work. Drill bits, like all tools, are made in various qualities. Carbon steel bits are cheap but essentially disposable. Buy high-speed steel bits for long life and accuracy. Some bits have coatings designed to improve performance.

■ **TWIST DRILLS** are the standard bits for making holes up to ½ inch in wood, plastic, metal, and other materials. Many new styles of twist drills cut faster and require less power, so they're well-suited to cordless drills. Reduced-shank drills allow you to use twist drills larger than the chuck capacity.

■ **BRAD-POINT DRILLS** have a sharpened point that makes starting in wood easier. Two spurs cut the hole before the bevels on the bit begin to remove material in the workpiece. Made in diameters from ⅛ to ¾ inch, these bits make drilling into endgrain easier.

■ **SPADE BITS** drill large holes—up to 1½ inches in diameter. They remove wood quickly, and their sharp tip guides the bit through the work.

■ **COUNTERBORE BITS,** for predrilling wood screws, bore the pilot hole, screw shank hole, and countersink or counterbore for the head all in one operation.

■ **HOLE SAWS** bore holes from 1 inch to 6 inches. A pilot bit centers the saw and guides the cutting edges of the saw. Use a side handle for sizes over 2 inches.

■ **MASONRY BITS** have carbide tips for boring holes in concrete, tile, brick, and other masonry materials.

SCREWDRIVING BITS

Screwdriving bits and holders are widely available. Buy a holder that accepts tips for slotted, phillips, square, and other screw heads.

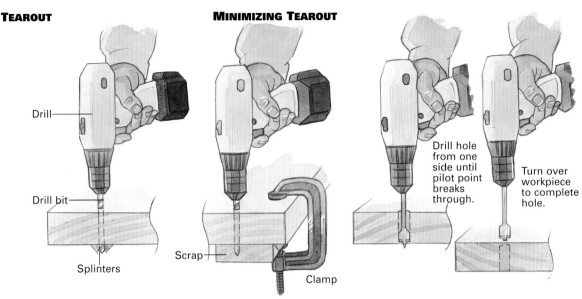

TEAROUT

Drill
Drill bit
Splinters

MINIMIZING TEAROUT

Scrap
Clamp

Drill hole from one side until pilot point breaks through.

Turn over workpiece to complete hole.

Drilling completely through a workpiece can splinter the wood as the bit breaks through the back.

Back the workpiece with scrap wood. A clamp will keep the scrap in contact as the bit breaks through the workpiece. Another method: Stop drilling just as the bit pokes through the workpiece. Flip the workpiece and drill from the other side.

DRILL/DRIVER SAFETY

Drill/drivers are relatively safe tools, but used unwisely, they can cause serious injury. Here are a few safety tips:
■ Always wear safety glasses/goggles when using a drill.
■ Keep your drill in good repair.
■ Insert bits and accessories fully into the chuck and tighten them firmly.
■ Clamp the workpiece whenever possible. Avoid securing it by hand. Don't let the bit bind in the workpiece.
■ With a keyed chuck, tighten the chuck in all three holes to equalize pressure on the shank of the bit.
■ Don't force the drill; allow its speed to do the work.
■ Use a side handle and hold the drill with two hands when drilling large holes.

DRILLING PILOT HOLES

Pilot Hole Diameter

Screw Gauge	Wood Screws		Production Screws	
	Hardwood	Softwood	Hardwood	Softwood
4	5/64"	1/16"	5/64"	1/16"
6	3/32"	5/64"	7/64"	3/32"
8	7/64"	3/32"	1/8"	7/64"
10	1/8"	7/64"	9/64"	1/8"
12	9/64"	1/8"	5/32"	9/64"
14	5/32"	9/64"	3/16"	5/32"

Drill through the top piece and into the bottom piece to a depth equal to the screw length. Clamp or hold the parts together as you drive in the screw.

USING A DRILL STAND

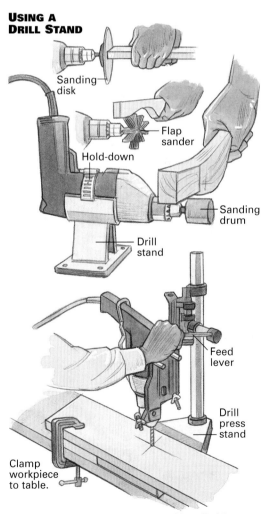

Sanding disk

Flap sander

Hold-down

Sanding drum

Drill stand

Feed lever

Drill press stand

Clamp workpiece to table.

Mount your drill in a stand to sand handheld pieces. Use fast speed and light pressure. Mount the drill in a drill press stand to make accurate or repetitive holes.

DRILL/DRIVER
continued

**DRILLING
STRAIGHT
HOLES**

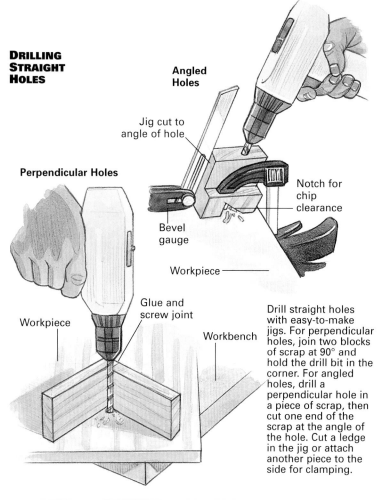

**Angled
Holes**

Jig cut to
angle of hole

Perpendicular Holes

Notch for
chip
clearance

Bevel
gauge

Workpiece

Workpiece

Glue and
screw joint

Workpiece

Workbench

Drill straight holes
with easy-to-make
jigs. For perpendicular
holes, join two blocks
of scrap at 90° and
hold the drill bit in the
corner. For angled
holes, drill a
perpendicular hole in
a piece of scrap, then
cut one end of the
scrap at the angle of
the hole. Cut a ledge
in the jig or attach
another piece to the
side for clamping.

ACCESSORIES

With the right accessories a drill can
accomplish an astonishing number of tasks.
A properly equipped drill can sand, grind,
polish, buff, clean materials, and drill
evenly spaced holes. The illustrations on
pages 14–17 show only a few of the jobs
you can accomplish.

USING YOUR POWER DRILL

Although a drill is one of the easiest tools to
use, here are some techniques that will make
your work go more smoothly.
■ Use a center punch to mark the center of
the hole. Set the tip of the bit in the punch
mark. Holding the drill with a firm grip, start
the drill at a slow speed. Increase speed as the
drill bites into the material.
■ Clamp the workpiece when possible and
use two hands on the drill. Use an auxiliary
handle, if you have one, for large holes. Use
light pressure and let the tool do the work.
■ Withdraw the bit often to remove chips.
■ Avoid tearout—the tendency of a bit to
splinter the wood as it breaks through the
opposite side of the hole—by using the
techniques shown on page 15.
■ Run the drill at the optimum speed.
Generally power goes up as speed goes
down—use high speed for thin metal and
slower speeds for thick wood.
■ Predrill holes for wood screws before
driving them. (See "Drilling Pilot Holes"
chart on page 15.)

**DEPTH
GUIDES**

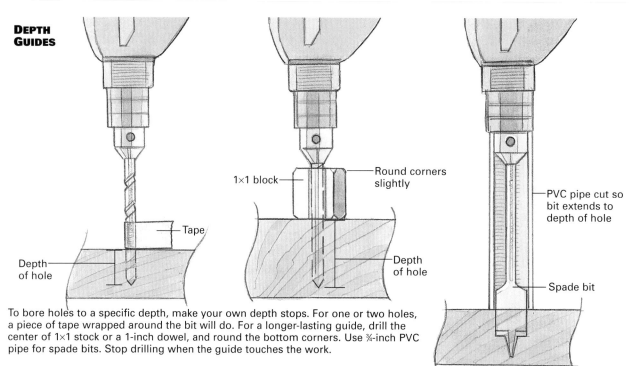

Tape

Depth
of hole

1×1 block

Round corners
slightly

Depth
of hole

PVC pipe cut so
bit extends to
depth of hole

Spade bit

To bore holes to a specific depth, make your own depth stops. For one or two holes,
a piece of tape wrapped around the bit will do. For a longer-lasting guide, drill the
center of 1×1 stock or a 1-inch dowel, and round the bottom corners. Use ¾-inch PVC
pipe for spade bits. Stop drilling when the guide touches the work.

DRIVING SCREWS

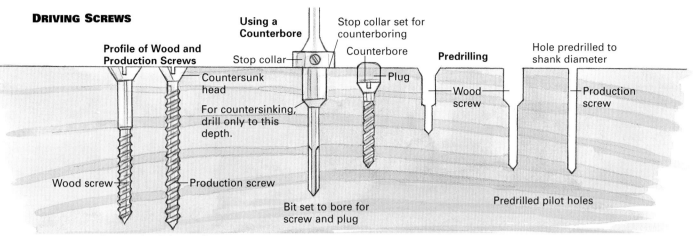

Profile of Wood and Production Screws

Using a Counterbore

Stop collar set for counterboring

Predrilling

Hole predrilled to shank diameter

Stop collar

Counterbore

Countersunk head

Plug

Wood screw

Production screw

For countersinking, drill only to this depth.

Wood screw

Production screw

Bit set to bore for screw and plug

Predrilled pilot holes

Wood screws have a shank larger than the threads. Production screws have the same size shank from tip to head. For wood screws, either predrill a separate pilot hole and shank hole or use a counterbore. Test the screw in a piece of scrap and set the clutch to slip when the screw reaches the right depth.

DRILLING METAL AND PLASTICS

Drilling metal and plastics requires techniques slightly different from drilling wood.

Always clamp the workpiece securely when drilling dense metals. Bits may tend to bind and spin the material. Start with a bit smaller than the final hole and center it in an indentation made with a punch. Start the drill at a slow speed and gradually increase it so the bit is removing material at a constant rate. Keep your feed rate constant. You will know when you've reached the optimum combination because the bit will turn out a steady ribbon of metal waste. For metal thicker than 1/8 inch, lubricate the drill with oil to keep it cool and running smoothly. Repeat the process with increasingly larger bits until the hole is the desired diameter.

Correct drill speed varies from material to material and with bit size. Generally, as the bit size increases, your drill speed should decrease. Spade bits with spurs are best for acrylic.

To drill thin stock, clamp the material between scrap blocks and drill into the scrap.

ENLARGING A HOLE

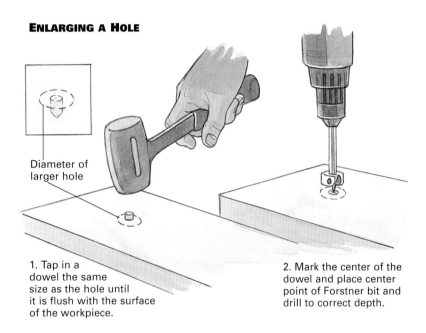

Diameter of larger hole

1. Tap in a dowel the same size as the hole until it is flush with the surface of the workpiece.

2. Mark the center of the dowel and place center point of Forstner bit and drill to correct depth.

CATCHING SAWDUST

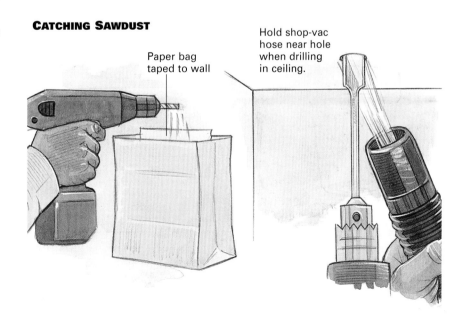

Paper bag taped to wall

Hold shop-vac hose near hole when drilling in ceiling.

CIRCULAR SAW

Aprofessional wouldn't think about building a house without a portable circular saw. And the tool is just as handy for do-it-yourself home maintenance and remodeling.

The circular saw lets you carry the tool to the work site—you don't need to haul studs, planks, or ¾-inch plywood sheets to the workshop, set up the radial arm saw or table saw, cut the materials, and carry them back to the job. Circular saws are made for speed and efficiency. You sacrifice a little precision compared to a table saw, but you can get surprisingly smooth, accurate cuts by using the right blade and a commercial or homemade cutting guide.

WHAT SIZE TO BUY?

Circular saws are sized by blade diameter. The most common saw—the one familiar to anyone who has ever watched a carpenter work or walked down the tool aisle of a hardware store—has a 7¼-inch blade. Smaller saws can often handle household repair and trim work, and their lighter weight makes them easier to handle. Most 6- or 6½-inch saws, for example, can cut 2× stock at 45 degrees in one pass. A saw with a 4½-inch blade (usually called a trim saw) will cut materials slightly thicker than 1 inch— adequate for sawing boards, moldings,

or sheet goods, but less useful for framing walls or other major construction projects.

Different blades and cutoff wheels allow you to cut materials other than wood— the largest variety of special blades fits the 7¼-inch model. This general-purpose size, available in a wide range of prices, represents the best choice for a home-use tool.

MOTORS AND MOUNTING

The motor on most circular saws is mounted crosswise to the base (helical-drive saws). On worm-drive saws, however, the motor is lengthwise on the base, as shown, below left. Some professionals prefer worm-drive models, believing they are better balanced over the cut. They are easier to use for many house-framing cuts too. Trim saws are often laid out this way for balance and compactness.

What about power? Your choices range from ½-hp models to heavy-duty saws with wood-munching 2½-hp motors. A 1-hp model equipped with the right blade will handle most do-it-yourself and home-maintenance chores without bogging down; just don't rush the tool when you're cutting.

GETTING A HANDLE ON YOUR SAW

The blade is usually to the right of the handle on helical-drive saws. Some manufacturers offer two versions of the same saw—one with the blade on the right and one with the blade on the left. The blade position can affect how easy it is for you to use the saw—left-handed people may find a saw with a left-side blade easier to use. Before you make your buy, pull the tool off the shelf to get an idea of how it feels in your hand. Is is too heavy? Does its balance feel

A worm-drive saw (left) is narrower and longer than a helical-drive saw (right). Worm-drive saws are usually heavier than the more common helical-drive models.

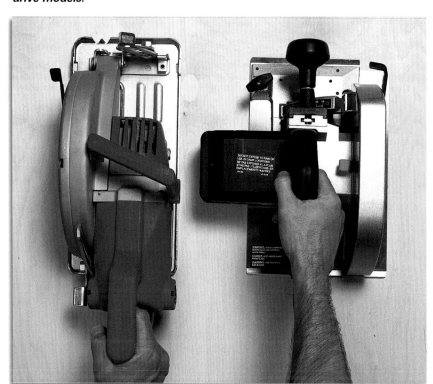

A CIRCULAR SAW CAN...

■ Rip and crosscut sheet goods to workable size
■ Rip and crosscut lumber to length and width
■ Plunge-cut openings for sinks, doors, and windows, and make other large openings
■ Cut bevels, miters, and chamfers with minimum setup
■ Cut lumber at a work site and with minimum setup

right? Can you see the sight line without straining? Make sure you get a saw that lets you see the blade; you'll get more accurate cuts if you can see what the blade is doing. All other things being equal, choose the saw that feels best. One that feels awkward will be hard to use and can cause safety hazards.

ADJUSTMENTS AND OTHER FEATURES

All circular saws feature two standard adjustments—cutting depth and angle. Other features, such as a blade brake, blade lock, and switch lock, are optional. More-expensive saws usually have more features.

■ **CUTTING DEPTH AND BEVEL ADJUSTMENTS:** On most models you set different cutting depths by adjusting the position of the saw plate. On these models, the blade and motor pivot at the front of the saw plate. On others, the motor and blade raise and lower above the plate, keeping the handle at a consistent angle no matter what the depth—a handy feature but not an essential one. To cut bevels, you tilt the motor and blade on the saw plate.

Make sure the adjustment controls are easy to reach, work smoothly, and lock positively. Look for easy-to-read bevel scales with markings from 0 to 50 degrees in 5-degree increments, a mark at 22½ degrees, and positive stops at 45 and 90 degrees.

■ **DEPTH ADJUSTMENT:** Easy-to-read depth scales are a plus, but not essential. Smooth operation and quick, positive depth locking are crucial.

■ **BLADE BRAKING:** You'll have to pay a little more for electric or electromagnetic braking, but this valuable safety feature stops the blade almost immediately after you release the trigger. It is worth the extra price.

■ **SWITCH LOCK:** Here's another feature that's worth the cost. It prevents accidental start-up of the saw; you need to press a button before you can squeeze the power switch.

■ **BLADE LOCK:** This is a less critical feature. A blade lock keeps the blade from turning, making blade changes easier. You can accomplish the same thing without cost by digging the blade into scrap stock before you put the wrench to the arbor bolt, as shown on page 21.

Look for a good balance between saw size and plate size—avoid saws with small plates or plates made from thin material. Saws with the blade guard lever about 2 inches above the plate are easier to maneuver when making plunge cuts than saws with levers positioned closer to the plate.

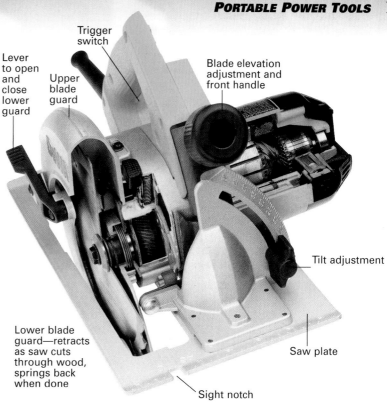

Trigger switch

Lever to open and close lower guard

Upper blade guard

Blade elevation adjustment and front handle

Tilt adjustment

Lower blade guard—retracts as saw cuts through wood, springs back when done

Saw plate

Sight notch

CORDED OR CORDLESS?

Circular saws are available as corded or cordless tools. Cordless saws are usually 6- or 6½-inch models or smaller trim saws. Often you'll find a cordless saw packaged in a kit with a cordless drill/driver and a spare battery. (Some kits include a flashlight or other tools.)

A cordless saw offers cut-anywhere portability, limited only by the duration of the battery's charge. (Manufacturers claim that a fully charged battery will make anywhere from 100 to 200 crosscuts in 2×4s.) They're not without drawbacks, however (see "Cordless Tools," page 7). Power and unlimited run time are advantages for corded saws.

WHAT DO THEY COST?

Corded circular saws start at about $35 and run into the hundreds of dollars for professional models. A few low-priced models sport some of the features (blade lock, for example) of higher-priced saws. However, if you're starting a major remodeling or construction project in which you'll give the saw heavy use, don't count on long life from a tool that costs about as much as a bag of groceries. You don't have to spend a fortune for a serviceable saw: You can get a high quality circular saw for about $120, and $150 or so (sometimes less) will get you a saw with a blade brake.

CIRCULAR SAW
continued

Combination blade (carbide-tipped)   Plywood blade with set teeth   Masonry blade

Rip blade (carbide-tipped)   Crosscut blade (carbide-tipped)   Fine-toothed combination blade (carbide-tipped)   Hollow-ground Plywood blade

CIRCULAR SAW BLADES

Ripping (cutting wood with the grain) and crosscutting (cutting across the grain) require saw blades with different kinds of teeth. Circular saws usually come equipped from the factory with a combination blade, which is adequate for general woodcutting. For more specialized work, you can install different kinds of blades. Here's a brief review of common circular saw blades.

■ **COMBINATION BLADE:** This general-purpose blade will rip cut and crosscut most woods without binding.

■ **CROSSCUT BLADE:** This blade is designed to make smooth crosscuts. Its teeth are sharpened and shaped for smooth passage across the grain.

■ **RIP BLADE:** Hooked teeth are the hallmark of this blade, designed to resist the tendency of wood fibers to close up and grab in rip cuts.

■ **PLYWOOD BLADE:** Many closely spaced teeth give smooth cuts with minimum splintering in plywood and veneered stock.

■ **HOLLOW-GROUND BLADE:** The blade body is thinner than the teeth, which are not set to the sides. This blade cuts smoothly and accurately, but more slowly than combination blades. It's ideal for cabinetry work.

■ **CARBIDE-TIPPED BLADES:** Available in many tooth styles, these blades have long-wearing carbide tips brazed to a steel blank.

Always buy the highest quality blade you can afford, preferably a carbide-tipped blade. A carbide-tipped blade holds its edge far

CHOOSING THE RIGHT BLADE

Material	Type of Cut	Blade to Use
Dry boards and dimensioned lumber	Ripping/crosscutting	16- to 20-tooth combination
	Rough cuts	12-tooth blade
	Smooth cuts	40-tooth blade or steel planer
Plywood, hardboard, and paneling	Ripping/crosscutting	16- to 20-tooth combination
	Smooth cuts	40-tooth blade, steel plywood blade or hollow-ground blade
Particleboard	Ripping/crosscutting	12-tooth blade (for quick cuts) or 16- to 20-tooth combination blade
	Smooth cuts	40-tooth blade
Lumber with nails	Ripping/crosscutting	Nail-cutting blade (flooring blade)
Laminate, plastics, and non-ferrous metals	Smooth cuts	40-tooth blade or abrasive-coated blade
Iron, Steel	General cutting	Abrasive edge for cutting steel
Masonry	General cutting	Abrasive edge for cutting masonry

All blades recommended are carbide tipped, unless otherwise noted.

longer between sharpenings. No matter what the purpose of the blade, look for smoothly ground teeth and smooth brazing.

Like other tool purchases, it's wise to buy saw blades as you need them. Always use blades for their intended purpose and keep them sharp and clean. The wrong blade or a dull one can burn wood surfaces, cause kickback, and overload your saw's motor.

ACCESSORIES

Miter guides, rip fences, and protractor guides are the most common accessories for circular saws. These guides increase the straightness and accuracy of your cuts, but most of the jobs done with commercial accessories can also be completed with homemade jigs or guides.

USING YOUR CIRCULAR SAW

When it comes to using a circular saw, start with the same rules that apply to all power tools: Take a firm grip, clamp the workpiece, and keep both hands on the saw if possible. From there, circular saws require a few techniques specific to their use.

■ **CUT WITH THE BACK SIDE UP:**
Measure and mark on the back of the stock and position the blade to make the cut on the waste side of your cut line. Sawing with the material's finished or good side down minimizes splintering on the good side. The upward-moving teeth at the front of the blade make the cut, splintering the side that's up.

■ **SET THE CUTTING DEPTH:** The blade should extend no more then ¼ inch through the thickness of the stock. Keep at least three teeth in the wood to minimize heat, reduce kickback, and keep the blade free of sawdust.

■ **LINE UP THE CUT:** Place the saw plate on the work, line up the guide on the cut line (or clamp guides to the work so the blade will fall on the line), turn the saw on and feed it into the work.

■ **SAWING IS NOT RACING:** Feed the saw into the work steadily and let the blade cut freely. Your feed speed will vary with the kind of material and its thickness.

■ **MINIMIZE KICKBACK:** Keep the kerf (the cut) open behind the blade in rip cuts with a kerf splitter (a piece of scrapwood or a commercial kerf splitter). This minimizes binding. If the saw binds, let the blade stop, move the saw back, and start again.

■ **STAND TO THE SIDE OF THE SAW:**
This will keep you out of the way of the saw in case it binds and kicks back. Do not stand directly behind the blade path.

Unplug the saw to install a new blade. Retract the guard and set the teeth firmly into a piece of scrap. Remove the bolt and replace the blade. Set the saw upside down with the blade at maximum cutting depth. Hold a square against the plate and blade and square the saw plate to the blade.

CIRCULAR-SAW SAFETY

A circular saw is the workhorse of home maintenance. Using it requires attention to safety practices.

■ When possible, avoid freehand cuts— clamp the workpiece to sawhorses or your worktable.

■ Wear safety goggles or glasses—the saw blade throws chips on the upstroke.

■ Keep the cord out of the saw's path and unplug it before changing a blade.

■ Avoid kickback. Let the saw come to full speed before the blade contacts the work, don't force the saw, use a kerf splitter when ripping, remove nails and fasteners before cutting, and keep the work well-supported. If the saw binds, let the blade stop spinning, back the saw up, and start again.

■ Work to the side of the saw, not directly behind it. Move your body instead of overextending your reach, and keep both hands on the saw whenever possible.

CIRCULAR SAW
continued

CROSSCUTTING WITH A CIRCULAR SAW

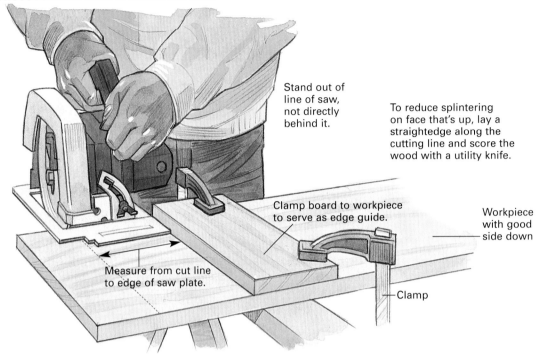

Stand out of line of saw, not directly behind it.

To reduce splintering on face that's up, lay a straightedge along the cutting line and score the wood with a utility knife.

Clamp board to workpiece to serve as edge guide.

Workpiece with good side down

Measure from cut line to edge of saw plate.

Clamp

CUTTING NONWOOD MATERIALS

Cutting laminates, metals, and masonry calls for different cutting techniques. Some materials require special blades (see "Choosing the Right Blade" on page 20).

■ **LAMINATES AND SOFT METALS (ALUMINUM, COPPER)** Use a fine-toothed, carbide-tipped blade and cut with the finished side down to keep the surface from chipping. Clamp laminate sheets and thin metals between plywood and clamp a guide to keep the cut straight. Laminate is brittle and will crack; metals can get caught in the blade.

■ **IRON AND STEEL** For roofing panels and thin-wall fence posts, use a carborundum or abrasive blade. For thicker plate materials, use an abrasive blade. Be prepared for plenty of sparks—wear safety goggles and don't saw near sawdust or flammable materials. Let the material cool before handling.

■ **MASONRY** A composition masonry blade will take care of most of your masonry sawing. If you're breaking concrete, saw slots ½ or ¾ inch deep into it, and then get out the sledge. For clean edges, rent a concrete saw with a diamond blade.

■ **USE GUIDES** whenever possible to keep the saw blade straight in the cut. You'll get more accurate cuts and keep the blade from binding, which harms the motor, heats up the blade, and can scorch the work.

■ **CUT THE STOCK, NOT THE CORD.** Always make sure the cord is completely out of the path of the blade. Slip it over your shoulder to keep it out of the way. Cut cords should not be spliced; replace them.

■ **WHEN MAKING FREEHAND CUTS,** lay the board on supports, clamp it in place, and guide the saw with two hands. Let the end hang past the supports so the cutoff piece can fall free.

MAINTAINING YOUR BLADES

Blades don't require much attention, until they become dull, but a few simple practices will reduce your sharpening chores.

■ **STORE** your blades in holders or racks with spacers between them. Blades stacked on the workbench will dull quickly as the metal surfaces wear against each other, and the edges of carbide teeth may become chipped. If your blades have to travel with you to a job site, carry them in a case.

■ **CLEAN** the pitch off your blades regularly. Pitch is resin or sap that accumulates from the wood fibers and hardens on the blade. If you

RIP CUTTING WITH A CIRCULAR SAW

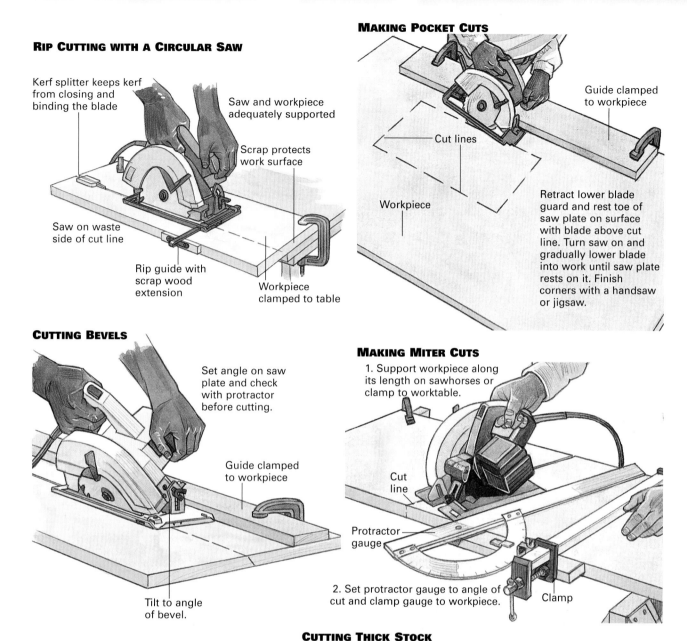

Kerf splitter keeps kerf from closing and binding the blade

Saw and workpiece adequately supported

Scrap protects work surface

Saw on waste side of cut line

Rip guide with scrap wood extension

Workpiece clamped to table

MAKING POCKET CUTS

Guide clamped to workpiece

Cut lines

Workpiece

Retract lower blade guard and rest toe of saw plate on surface with blade above cut line. Turn saw on and gradually lower blade into work until saw plate rests on it. Finish corners with a handsaw or jigsaw.

CUTTING BEVELS

Set angle on saw plate and check with protractor before cutting.

Guide clamped to workpiece

Tilt to angle of bevel.

MAKING MITER CUTS

1. Support workpiece along its length on sawhorses or clamp to worktable.

Cut line

Protractor gauge

2. Set protractor gauge to angle of cut and clamp gauge to workpiece.

Clamp

CUTTING THICK STOCK

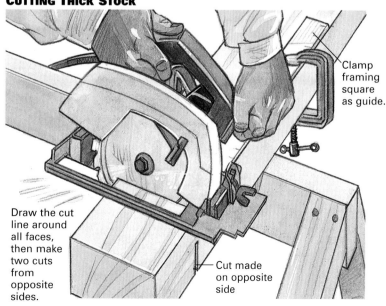

Clamp framing square as guide.

Draw the cut line around all faces, then make two cuts from opposite sides.

Cut made on opposite side

leave it on, it increases friction and heat retention within the cut. You can get it off with commercial pitch removers, oven cleaners, or spray surface cleaners, but don't use abrasives—they scratch and make subsequent pitch removal more difficult. A brass brush works well for cleaning blades.

■ **SHARPEN** your blades when they become dull. Burning, slow cuts, and a tendency for the blade to climb out of the stock rather than cut through it are signs the blade is dull. You could sharpen high-speed steel blades yourself with a file, but sharpening is precision work and is usually best done by a professional. An improperly sharpened blade will not make straight, accurate cuts and could be unbalanced enough to damage the saw. Carbide-tipped blades should always be sent to a professional sharpener.

JIGSAW

A jigsaw (sometimes called a saber saw) is one of the most versatile shop tools. It will make both straight and curved cuts, plunge into thick wood, and cut bevels and angles, all with minimal setup. It will cut a wide range of materials too.

Along with a cordless drill and circular saw, a jigsaw ranks as a workshop essential. If you're not going to be doing a lot of framing work with 2× lumber, a jigsaw may be the only power saw you need. A jigsaw will do many of the jobs normally done by a circular saw—cutting wide shelf boards to length, for instance—albeit more slowly. If your shop work is light and your budget is tight, get the jigsaw first and buy a circular saw when you need one.

Jigsaws are widely available and range from light-duty, single-speed models to high-quality, variable-speed machines with adjustable blade action.

THE SAW THAT FEELS RIGHT

When shopping for a jigsaw, look at those with at least a 3-amp motor. Hold each saw as you would when using it to see how it feels in your hand. The feel depends in part on its handle style—you'll find top-handle, barrel-grip, and in-line jigsaws.

Top-handle models are the most common. With a barrel-grip saw, you hang onto the cylindrical motor housing. This reduces the tendency to tilt the saw in corners, some say. In-line saws are similar to barrel-grip models, except the blade extends from the end of the motor housing—like a small reciprocating saw (see page 29). A heavier saw will probably vibrate less when you're making a cut.

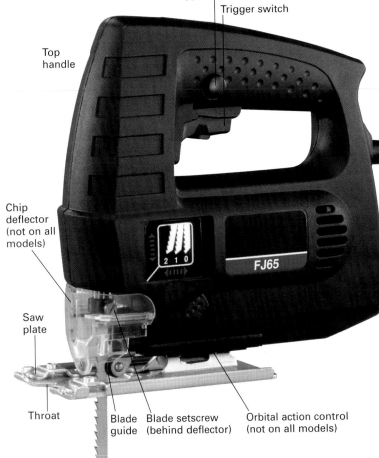

Trigger lock
Trigger switch
Top handle
Chip deflector (not on all models)
Saw plate
Throat
Blade guide
Blade setscrew (behind deflector)
Orbital action control (not on all models)

FJ65

SPEED, STROKE LENGTH, AND ACTION

Consider these factors when you shop:

■ **VARIABLE SPEED:** A variable-speed saw is more versatile. Once you get the saw home, you'll discover a host of uses for it. Many of those jobs will call for different speeds. A variable-speed range of 500 to 3,000 strokes per minute will handle most of your needs, whether you're cutting thin wood, thick wood, metal, ceramic tiles, or other materials.

■ **BLADE STROKE LENGTH:** This affects both how fast the saw will cut and how smooth the cut will be. A saw with a 1-inch stroke will cut faster and cleaner, but you can get satisfactory results with a ¾-inch stroke.

■ **ORBITAL ACTION:** An orbital-action blade moves forward on the cutting (up) stroke and backward on the downstroke, which helps clear sawdust from the cut and the blade. A saw with orbital action can cut about twice as fast as a nonorbital saw with the same motor power. Orbital motion is usually adjustable and can be turned off for tight curves or delicate work. It's not available on all saws.

ADJUSTABLE SAW PLATE

A tilting saw plate lets you cut bevels. Look for a clearly marked guide and positive locking at 45 and 90 degrees. This is handy, especially if you use the saw in place of a circular saw. An adjustable saw plate is standard on most saws above basic models.

OTHER FEATURES

Prices increase with the number of saw features. Depending on your budget and your use of the saw, some may be worth it.

■ **CHANGING BLADES:** Look for the quickest blade-change mechanism you can afford. Manufacturers have made many improvements in blade chucks—one actually pops the blade out to make changing a breeze. For the traditional setscrew blade chuck, the screw should be easy to get at. Select a saw that will accept the kind of blade you will use—the universal style is most common.

■ **DUST PORT:** A jigsaw doesn't spew out the volume of dust a circular saw does. But sawdust can obscure the cutting line, making it difficult to complete an intricate cut. To pick up sawdust as you cut, buy a saw that has a connection port for a shop-vacuum or dust-collection hose.

■ **SCROLLING:** This feature lets you change the direction of the cut by turning a knob, not the saw body. It's useful when cutting tight curves or sawing in a place that restricts saw movement.

CORDED OR CORDLESS?

Unlike power drills, you probably won't need both a corded and cordless jigsaw. Aside from convenience, the chief argument for a cordless model is that jigsaws are not usually used for long periods at a time. If you buy a cordless saw, be sure to buy two batteries.

COST

Prices for jigsaws range from about $30 for a low-power saw with few features to more than $450 for a cordless, 18-volt saw. You can get a good 4-amp saw with an adjustable plate, variable speeds, orbital action, and a dust port for a little more than $60. This kind of saw will serve well for occasional use. Saws in the $120 to $160 range have more powerful motors and all the features available, including toolless blade changing. These higher-price models usually withstand heavier use too.

A JIGSAW CAN...

■ Crosscut and rip stock to width and length with little setup
■ Cut curves and inside corners
■ Plunge-cut openings for pipes, sinks, electrical outlets, and other fixtures or saw corners of cutouts made with a circular saw
■ Cut scrollwork, angles, and bevels—in tight corners

JIGSAW SAFETY

Jigsaws are easy to use and rank as one of the safest power tools. To stay safe, follow these practices.

■ Clamp the workpiece as close to the cut line as possible, and use both hands on the saw whenever you can.
■ Wear safety glasses or goggles. Wear a dust mask if you're going to be kicking up a lot of dust.
■ Rest the saw plate on the work and allow the blade to come to full speed before starting the cut.
■ Keep the cord—and your fingers—out of the way of the blade.
■ Don't force the blade—a snapped blade can become a projectile.
■ Use the right blade for the material, and make sure it's sharp.
■ Let the blade cool when you're finished cutting—sawing can heat up the blade enough to burn your fingers.

JIGSAW
continued

BLADES

Toothless blade— abrasive edge

Reverse-tooth blade

Flush-cutting blade

Hollow-ground wood blade

Toothless blade— knife edge

Wave-set metal-cutting blade

Shank Styles

Tang shank

Universal shank

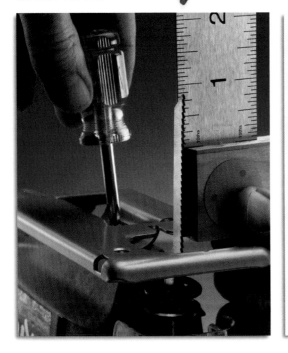

Square the blade to the base plate with a try square for accurate cuts.

JIGSAW BLADES

Blade choice accounts for much of the jigsaw's versatility. In general, the fewer teeth per inch (tpi) on the blade, the faster and coarser the cut. Wide blades are best for straight cuts. Narrow ones (¼ inch or less) are best suited to curves but will break more easily. Pick the coarsest blade that will allow you to keep three teeth in the material all the time. Jigsaw blades are cheap, and the price of an extra pack could save your having to make another trip to the hardware store in the middle of a project. Here are some common blades.

■ **COMBINATION BLADE:** This all-purpose blade will make straight and curved cuts with moderate speed and smoothness.

■ **FLUSH-CUTTING BLADE:** The teeth on this blade extend to the front of the saw plate to allow cuts up to a perpendicular surface.

■ **REVERSE-TOOTH BLADE:** This one cuts on the downstroke, reducing splintering on the top surface of veneers and plywood. It tries to lift the saw with each stroke, though.

■ **WAVE-SET METAL-CUTTING BLADE:** Very fine teeth and a wavy edge like a hacksaw blade identify this blade made for cutting metal and veneers.

■ **HOLLOW-GROUND WOOD BLADE:** The teeth are not set to the sides on this blade, so it makes smoother, finer cuts than a blade with set teeth.

■ **TOOTHLESS BLADE:** There are two kinds of toothless blades. One type has a knife

CHOOSING THE RIGHT JIGSAW BLADE

Type of Material/Cut	Blades (teeth per inch)
Thick wood/fast, rough cuts	3-7 tpi
Hardwood, softwood, plastics/general use	10 tpi
Plywood, veneer, laminates/ smooth cuts	10-tpi taper-ground blade, reverse-tooth blade, or toothless tungsten-carbide blade
Aluminum, copper, brass	up to ¼", general use 6-10 tpi, 14 tpi for smooth cuts
Thin sheet metal and tubing/ smooth cuts	24 tpi wave-set metal-cutting blade
Iron or steel pipe, rod, and bar stock	32 tpi wave-set metal-cutting blade
Rubber, leather, drywall, cloth, acrylic tiles	Toothless knife blade
Ceramic tile, slate, masonry	Carbide-edge abrasive blade
Small logs	3-7 tpi (6 inches long)

CROSSCUTTING WITH A JIGSAW

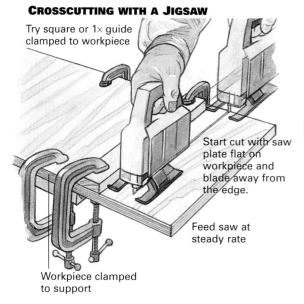

Try square or 1× guide clamped to workpiece

Start cut with saw plate flat on workpiece and blade away from the edge.

Feed saw at steady rate

Workpiece clamped to support

RIP CUTTING WITH AN EDGE GUIDE

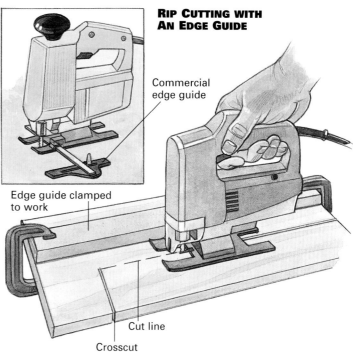

Commercial edge guide

Edge guide clamped to work

Cut line

Crosscut

edge for cutting a fine line in leather, rubber, and soft plastics. Another kind has an edge coated with tungsten carbide or diamond abrasive grit for cutting ceramics, masonry, and other hard materials.

ACCESSORIES AND JIGS

Although you'll probably do most of your jigsaw work without accessories, or with

ROTARY CUTOUT TOOL

A rotary cutout tool does much the same work as a jigsaw. However, by cutting with a rotating bit instead of a reciprocating blade, the cutout tool makes many cuts better. It is the handiest, quickest, and most accurate device for cutting holes in drywall or plaster. It makes short work of cutting holes in many materials, even ceramic tile, as shown above. For construction or remodeling work, consider adding one of these to your tool kit.

homemade guides, commercial edge guides and circle-cutting jigs are available.

An antisplintering plate is available for some saws. Made of plastic, it fits close to the blade in the saw plate throat to minimize tearout on the upper surface when cutting wood. You can minimize splintering by clamping thin scrapwood to the top of the workpiece or cutting on the back side.

CUTTING NONWOOD MATERIALS

Your jigsaw isn't just for wood. It will cut any metal faster and with less effort than a hacksaw. It also helps you reach cuts you couldn't make with a hacksaw because its frame gets in the way. Here are some tips that can make working with nonwood materials trouble-free.

■ **FOR THIN STOCK,** clamp the material between thin sheets of plywood. When clamping is impractical—on rain gutters and downspouts, fiberglass, and roof panels, for example—hold tight, cut slowly, and use a toothless blade.

■ **WHEN SAWING METALS,** it will pay to run a thin line of oil down the cut, or lubricate the blade with a grease stick to keep it from clogging and overheating.

■ **SYNTHETIC COUNTERTOP MATERIAL** cuts well with wood-cutting blades, but use fine teeth (or a toothless blade) to keep it from chipping.

■ **FOR PLEXIGLASS,** use a fine-toothed blade and cut slowly to avoid melting the plastic. Keep the protective film on the plastic until you're finished cutting.

JIGSAW
continued

USING YOUR JIGSAW

Jigsaw operation is fairly straightforward, even on curved cuts.

■ Clamp the work securely, putting the finish or good side down, unless you're going to use a reverse-tooth blade.

■ Keep the area under the workpiece clear of obstructions.

■ Clamp guides to the work for straight cuts, or use a commercial edge guide.

■ Except when making plunge cuts, set the saw plate flat on the work and start the saw before pushing the blade into the work.

■ Keep a firm grip on the tool and apply slight downward pressure to reduce vibration—the chief cause of poor cuts and broken blades.

■ Keep the saw plate flat on the workpiece.

■ Use the right saw speed for the work. Generally, you should use slower saw speeds with coarser blades, and faster speeds with finer blades.

■ Feed the saw into the work at a steady rate that allows the blade to cut freely.

■ Use relief cuts when cutting along tight curves. (See illustration below.)

■ If your blade tends to wander in the cut, especially in a turn, the blade may be too thin for the job, the teeth on one side may be dull, or you may be pushing the blade into the work too fast. Change the blade or slow down the feed rate.

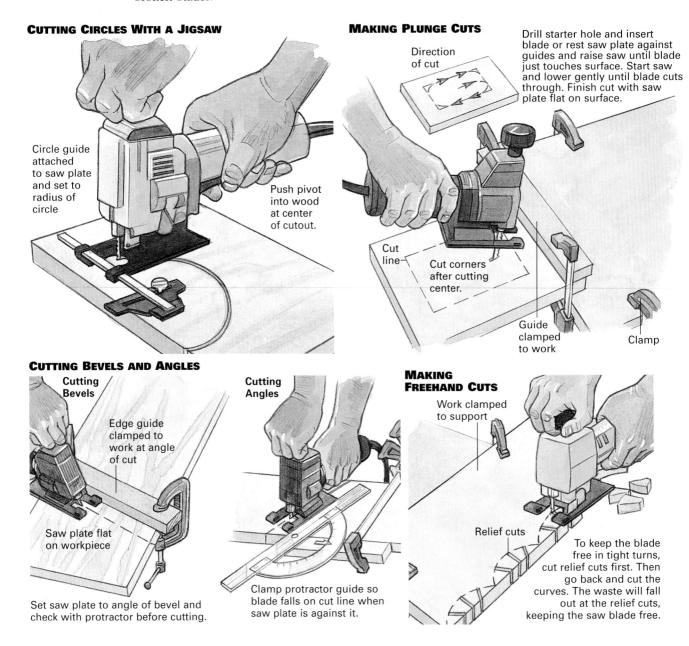

CUTTING CIRCLES WITH A JIGSAW

Circle guide attached to saw plate and set to radius of circle

Push pivot into wood at center of cutout.

MAKING PLUNGE CUTS

Direction of cut

Drill starter hole and insert blade or rest saw plate against guides and raise saw until blade just touches surface. Start saw and lower gently until blade cuts through. Finish cut with saw plate flat on surface.

Cut line

Cut corners after cutting center.

Guide clamped to work

Clamp

CUTTING BEVELS AND ANGLES

Cutting Bevels

Edge guide clamped to work at angle of cut

Saw plate flat on workpiece

Set saw plate to angle of bevel and check with protractor before cutting.

Cutting Angles

Clamp protractor guide so blade falls on cut line when saw plate is against it.

MAKING FREEHAND CUTS

Work clamped to support

Relief cuts

To keep the blade free in tight turns, cut relief cuts first. Then go back and cut the curves. The waste will fall out at the relief cuts, keeping the saw blade free.

RECIPROCATING SAW

A reciprocating saw is the beefy big brother of a jigsaw. Its action is essentially the same as a jigsaw's, except the stroke is longer, the blade is heavier, and the motor is more powerful. That makes it especially useful for demolition work. Its in-line design lets it reach into tight spaces.

If you're cutting the bottoms of wall studs (complete with nails) to remove a wall, making a new door opening in lath and plaster, or sawing through the roof for a new skylight, this is the tool for the job. And there are blades made for just about any material you need to cut.

Most reciprocating saws cost $150 to $200. Saws that are available for slightly more than $100 usually have plenty of power, adequate stroke length, and variable speeds for occasional do-it-yourself jobs.

There are plenty of special-purpose blades on the market, but the ones shown above right will handle most of your chores. A carbide-grit blade, available in several lengths, is the one to use for cutting cast iron, ceramic tile, and stainless steel.

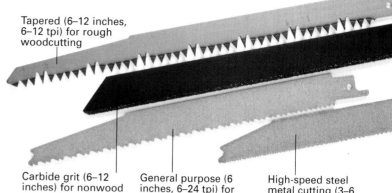

Tapered (6–12 inches, 6–12 tpi) for rough woodcutting

Carbide grit (6–12 inches) for nonwood materials

General purpose (6 inches, 6–24 tpi) for most wood and wood products

High-speed steel metal cutting (3–6 inches, 10–24 tpi) for cutting heavy metal stock

A RECIPROCATING SAW CAN...

■ Cut through walls, sheathing, subfloors, pipes, and studs to remove material for demolition work
■ Cut openings for outlets, pipes, doors, and windows
■ Crosscut and rip stock, cut straight cuts and curves, angles and bevels, plunge cuts and circles

With a long blade you can cut through walls. Make sure the blade is at least 2 inches longer than the wall thickness. For blind cuts, use a blade 2 inches shorter than the wall thickness so its tip won't hit the inside of the opposite face.

RECIPROCATING-SAW SAFETY

This saw demands two-hand control or it will buck away from the work, snap the blade, and possibly lurch into adjacent surfaces or the operator. In addition, you should always:
■ Wear heavy-duty safety goggles or glasses. Reciprocating saws can throw large chips of debris at surprising velocities.
■ Keep the saw plate on the work.
■ Check walls for electrical wiring or plumbing lines before you cut into them.
■ Let the blade cool before touching it or changing it.
■ Keep the cord out of the line of the blade.
■ Unplug the saw when changing blades.

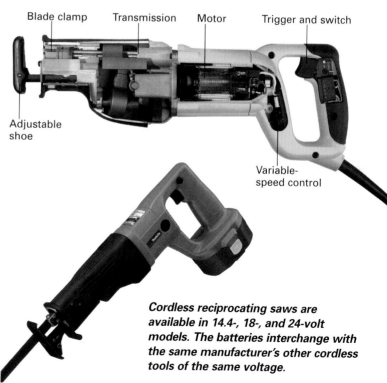

Blade clamp   Transmission   Motor   Trigger and switch

Adjustable shoe

Variable-speed control

Cordless reciprocating saws are available in 14.4-, 18-, and 24-volt models. The batteries interchange with the same manufacturer's other cordless tools of the same voltage.

SANDERS

Sanders have one job to do—remove surface defects and leave the surface smooth for the final finish.

There are three kinds of portable power sanders—belt sanders, orbital sanders, and random-orbit sanders. Orbital and random-orbit sanders are often called finish sanders.

WHICH SANDER DO I NEED?

Finishing a wood surface requires the following steps:
■ removing saw and other mill marks,
■ preliminary smoothing,
■ final smoothing,
■ sanding between finish coats.

The kind of sander you buy will depend on the work you intend to do. You will need more than one type of sander to do all the finishing steps.

■ **BELT SANDER:** A belt sander's weight, powerful motor, aggressive sanding action, and large sanding surface make it ideal for removing wood in a hurry. It's the tool to use when you are preparing a surface for finish sanding, removing mill marks from wide stock, or leveling glued-up edges.

Change to another sander for finish sanding—the finest-grit sanding belt is too rough for finish sanding, and the machine is too bulky for finish work.

■ **ORBITAL SANDER:** This sander moves the abrasive sheet in tiny orbits at high speed, which suits it well to finish sanding. An orbital sander will take off blemishes and mill marks on large surfaces, but not nearly as fast as the belt sander. You can reduce the tool's tendency to leave swirl marks by using top-quality papers and sanding carefully. Sanding across the grain with one—at the corners of a picture frame, for example—leaves a small swirled trail. Orbital sanders commonly use one-half, one-third, or one-fourth of a sheet of sandpaper. Detail sanders (see page 34) are orbital sanders designed for use in corners.

■ **RANDOM-ORBIT SANDER:** This tool found its way into woodworking from the auto-body field. Random-orbit sanders have a circular sanding pad that rotates and moves in random elliptical orbits at the same time. This leaves a swirl-free surface, as long as you keep the sander flat on the work.

For fast, rough work over larger surfaces, nothing beats a belt sander. A palm-grip random-orbit sander excels at fine sanding.

A BELT SANDER CAN...

■ Quickly sand off large amounts of wood on flat surfaces
■ Remove paint and other finishes
■ Smooth vertical and horizontal surfaces
■ Prepare surfaces for finish sanding
■ Smooth uneven joints to a uniform height
■ With a stand, sand small objects

SANDER ACTIONS

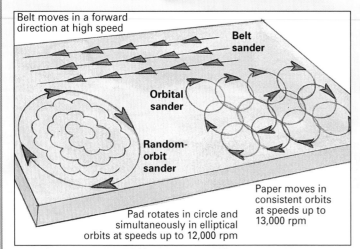

Belt moves in a forward direction at high speed

Belt sander

Orbital sander

Random-orbit sander

Pad rotates in circle and simultaneously in elliptical orbits at speeds up to 12,000 rpm

Paper moves in consistent orbits at speeds up to 13,000 rpm

Each type of sander produces distinctively different sanding actions, each designed for a specific kind of sanding. A belt sander's abrasive moves forward only, which suits it for fast removal of stock and rough sanding. An orbital sander makes a smooth surface, but can leave minute swirl marks that show up in the finish. The motion of a random-orbit sander produces the finest, most swirl-free finish.

Buy at least these two if your budget will support the cost. If you are limited to one model, get a pistol-grip random-orbit sander. It can handle the rough work, and is also capable of leaving your finishes smooth as glass.

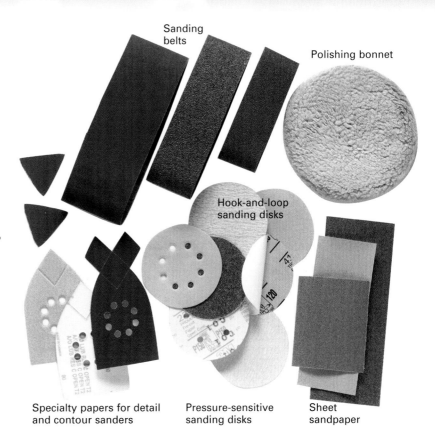

Sanding belts

Polishing bonnet

Hook-and-loop sanding disks

Specialty papers for detail and contour sanders

Pressure-sensitive sanding disks

Sheet sandpaper

GETTING A GRIP

Belt sanders usually have two handles, as shown on the opposite page. Finish sanders come with several handle configurations.
■ **PISTOL GRIP:** This style has front and rear handles for two-hand use. (See page 33.)
■ **PALM GRIP:** This sander is designed to be held in one hand. (See page 33.)
■ **BARREL HANDLE:** Based on a handheld grinder, this type of handle is found mostly on heavy-duty random-orbit sanders.

SANDER ACTIONS

Each type of sander is designed for a specific kind of sanding. The belt sander's belt moves forward only, which suits it for fast removal of stock and rough sanding. An orbital sander produces a smooth surface, but can leave tiny swirl marks that show up in the finish. The dual action of a random-orbit sander produces the finest, most swirl-free finish.

SANDER SAFETY

Both orbital and random-orbit sanders are relatively safe tools that don't pose much potential for injury. Wear a dust mask with all sanders and let them stop before resting them on other surfaces.
Belt sanders require special attention.
■ Always use a stop block or clamps to keep the belt from throwing the work.
■ Always hold a belt sander with both hands.

CHOOSING THE RIGHT ABRASIVE

Application	Tool(s) to Use	Abrasive Type	Grit
Surfacing rough wood, fast stock removal	Random-orbit or belt sander	Aluminum oxide or zirconia alumina	36–80
Removing mill marks, saw marks, defects, sanding end grain	Random-orbit, orbital, or belt sander	Aluminum oxide, zirconia alumina, or garnet	60–100
Smooth sanding	Random-orbit or orbital sander, or hand sanding with sheet sandpaper, sanding blocks, or medium-fine nonwoven pads	Aluminum oxide, garnet, or silicon carbide	120–320
Sanding contours	Detail or contour sander / Sanding blocks, nonwoven pads	Aluminum oxide, garnet, or silicon carbide / Aluminum oxide or silicon carbide	80–320 / Coarse-fine

Sanding does not need to proceed through every grit. For rough sanding use a grit in the 80–100 range. Switch to a finishing sander with 150–180-grit paper, and complete the job with a 220-grit paper.

SANDERS
continued

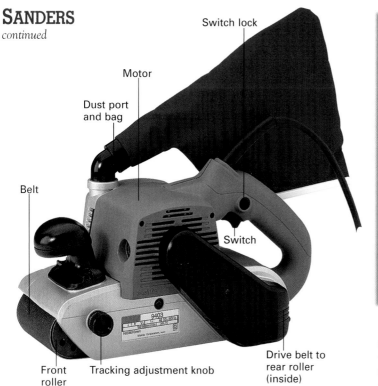

Switch lock

Motor

Dust port
and bag

Belt

Switch

Front
roller

Tracking adjustment knob

Drive belt to
rear roller
(inside)

BELT SANDER

This workhorse has been around for a long time. Most belt sanders look nearly alike, with only minor variations among models.

Belt sanders are designated by their belt size (width × length). Sizes range from 2½×16 inches to 4×24 inches. A midsize sander (3×21 or 24 inches) offers enough flexibility to meet most of your needs.

Belt speeds top out at about 1,600 rpm, and variable-speed models allow a little more control of the tool. Once you get the hang of a single-speed sander, however, you probably won't miss speed control. Always start the tool first, and then lay the sander gently on the work. Maintain a firm grip and keep the sander moving to prevent gouges.

Power and weight go hand in hand. A 6- to 8-amp model is a good choice for home-workshop use. Such a sander will weigh about 8 pounds, heavy enough for the job but not so heavy it will physically wear you out.

Belt sanders can take off ¼ inch of wood quickly. They generate more dust than almost any other tool, so a dust-collection port is a plus and is worth the cost.

Heavyweight belt sanders cost more than $200. Midsize models that meet normal do-it-yourself needs are available for around $100.

USING A BELT SANDER

Clamp light to worktable to inspect surface.

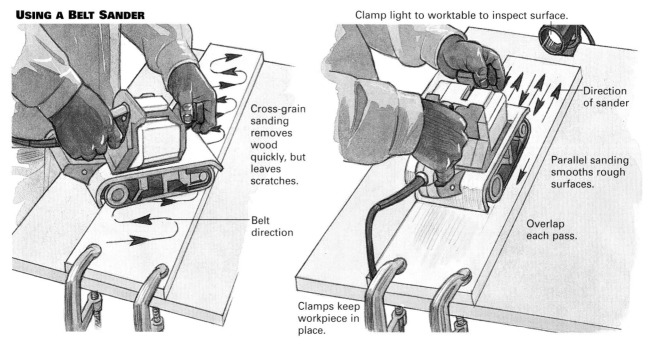

Cross-grain sanding removes wood quickly, but leaves scratches.

Belt direction

Direction of sander

Parallel sanding smooths rough surfaces.

Overlap each pass.

Clamps keep workpiece in place.

ORBITAL SANDERS

Before the advent of random-orbit sanders, orbital sanders were called *finishing sanders*. They still are, although that term now applies to both. Made in sizes that take one-half, one-third, or one-quarter sheet of sandpaper, orbital sanders produce a fine finish with only one potential drawback—small swirl marks. They're the perfect tool, however, for quickly sanding surfaces in preparation for final sanding with a random-orbit sander.

Handle styles vary from model to model and with sheet size. The third- and half-sheet sanders usually have a pistol-grip handle and more power. Although made for fine work, larger orbital sanders will do their fair share of rough sanding also. The smaller quarter-sheet models won't work as fast, but their light weight and comfortable handle offer more control and better access in tight spaces, and they are less tiring to use.

Orbital sanders come with variable speeds, noise and vibration reduction, and dust ports. All three are worthwhile features. You can get a good quality quarter-sheet orbital sander for $50 to $70 and a one-third-sheet version for about $90. The price increases for half-sheet models; expect to pay between $120 and $150.

PISTOL-GRIP SANDER — Handle, Sandpaper-retaining clip, Trigger switch, Dust port and bag, Pad

PALM-GRIP SANDER — Power switch, Sandpaper-retaining clip, Pad

AN ORBITAL SANDER CAN...

- Smooth surfaces and protective finishes
- Smooth wood to accept stains and finish

CHANGING PAPER

Sandpaper retaining clip

- With the sander on end, release the paper-retaining clips from one end (or retract the clamps on some models), pull out the old sheet, and repeat for the other end.
- Using a paper cut to the correct size, push one end under the retainers as far as the edge will go. Square the paper on the pad and hook the clips.
- Fold the paper around the end of the pad and work it into the retainers at the other side. With the paper tight, rehook the clips.

USING AN ORBITAL SANDER

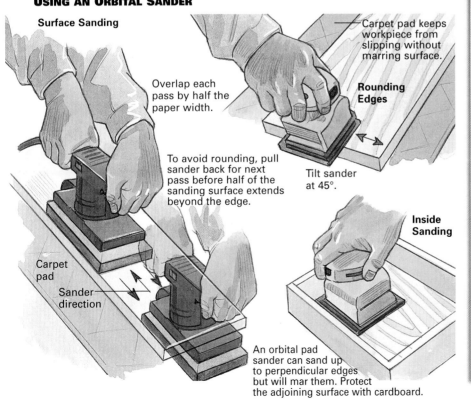

Surface Sanding — Overlap each pass by half the paper width. To avoid rounding, pull sander back for next pass before half of the sanding surface extends beyond the edge. Carpet pad. Sander direction.

Rounding Edges — Carpet pad keeps workpiece from slipping without marring surface. Tilt sander at 45°.

Inside Sanding — An orbital pad sander can sand up to perpendicular edges but will mar them. Protect the adjoining surface with cardboard.

SANDERS
continued

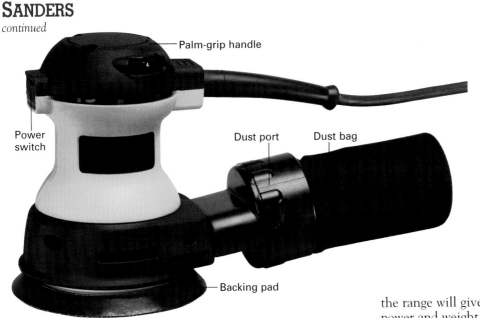

Palm-grip handle

Power switch

Dust port

Dust bag

Backing pad

A RANDOM-ORBIT SANDER CAN...

- Smooth surfaces and protective finishes at high speeds without swirl marks
- Flatten joints to a uniform surface
- Sand cross-grain joints
- Smooth wood for stains and finishes

RANDOM-ORBIT SANDERS

Although some models come with variable speed controls that let you make adjustments for the grit and material you're sanding, this is a feature you might forgo if it pushes the price out of your range.

Dust collection is a standard feature, pulling the dust through holes in the paper and pad. And you're better off hooking the sander to your dust-collection system rather than relying on the small bag attached. These sanders produce fine dust, and aside from the potential hazard to your lungs, the dust can obscure your view of the work.

You'll find power in a range from 1.4 to 5.5 amps and speeds from about 8,000 to 13,000 orbits per minute. Sanders in the middle of

the range will give you a good balance of power and weight. Buy the highest speed you can afford, and choose the sander that feels best in your hand.

Expect to pay $50 to $70 for a palm-grip model, and from $120 to $150 for a heftier barrel-grip right-angle sander.

DETAIL AND CONTOUR SANDERS

Detail sanders allow you to sand where no other sander will go. The detail sander's triangular platen (some have slightly different shapes) let you sand right up to a perpendicular surface. The point will reach into narrow spaces. Contour sanders make it easy to sand moldings or shaped work. (See the photos on the opposite page.)

When you have to sand window frames, tight stair corners, furniture, or moldings,

USING A RANDOM-ORBIT SANDER

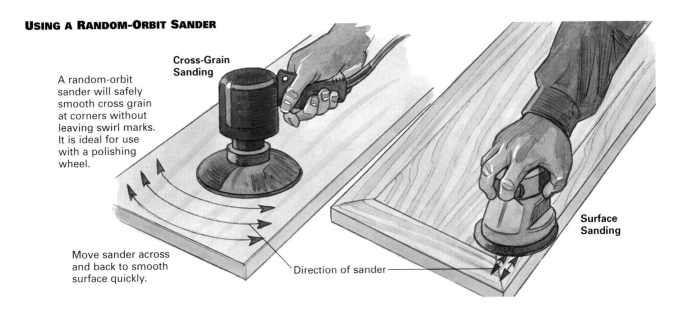

Cross-Grain Sanding

A random-orbit sander will safely smooth cross grain at corners without leaving swirl marks. It is ideal for use with a polishing wheel.

Move sander across and back to smooth surface quickly.

Direction of sander

Surface Sanding

these specialty sanders help take the frustration out of the work.

Detail sanders have either oscillating or orbital action. From the outside, both types look pretty much the same; the difference is in the sanding motion of the tool. The head on an oscillating model swings back and forth in an arc. Orbiters work like finishing sanders, their pads rotating in tight circles. Oscillating sanders are easier to control, but prone to leave marks. Orbital models are less likely to mark the work, but can chatter off the surface. Speeds are given in strokes per minute (spm) or oscillations per minute (opm).

Many, but not all, contour sanders sand like you would with a sanding block—back and forth in a straight line. But they do it at about 6,000 strokes per minute. The sander uses hollow or solid rubber profiles that are wrapped with pressure-sensitive sandpaper (hook-and-loop on some models) to smooth out almost any shape. And if the stock contours don't suit you, you can shape the solid pads with a sharp knife.

COST

Look for detail sanders in the $75 to $100 range. Contour sanders cost from $100 to $150. Your chief consideration in shopping for a detail or contour sander should be how many times you'll take the sander out of the storage cabinet. If you frequently do refinishing or other projects that involve lots of moldings and other shaped surfaces, you may use the tool often. It could be worth the cost—considering time and effort saved— to buy one of these specialty sanders for a single large project.

The 3D contour sander's three pivoting platens (inset above) conform to curved surfaces, such as this chair seat.

The contour sander's shaped pads (left) are ideal for sanding moldings and curved surfaces.

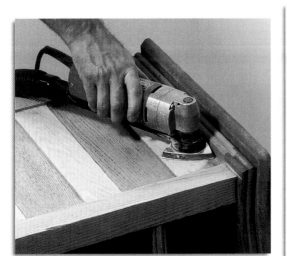

A detail sander sands into tight spots without marring adjacent surfaces.

CHANGING PAPER

Sandpaper attaches to a random-orbit sander with either pressure-sensitive adhesive or hook-and-loop material. To replace either one, peel the old paper off the sander, then put on the new one, starting at one edge and applying light pressure over the surface. Many sanders have dust ports in the pad; buy paper that has the same number of holes. Align the holes in the paper with the holes in the backup pad.

ROUTER

Edge guide

Stop block clamped to workpiece

You can easily cut decorative grooves for furniture or moldings with a plunge router. Stop blocks keep the groove lengths uniform.

Little more than a motor spinning a bit, a router is a simple tool. Yet it is probably the most versatile tool you can add to your shop. It's most often used for shaping the edges of a workpiece—rounding, rabbeting, chamfering, or adding decorative molding patterns. But it's also adept at carving out grooves and dadoes, making signs, trimming parts to a template, carving surface designs, and making a wide range of strong and attractive joints. A router can be handheld or mounted in a table.

Depth adjustment ring

Handle

Collet
Subbase
Base plate

FIXED-BASE OR PLUNGE?

Two router styles are available—fixed-base and plunge routers. With a fixed-base router, bit protrusion past the base plate is fixed. In a plunge router, the motor is spring-loaded on two columns, which lets you keep the plate flat on the work and push the bit down into it. Both styles let you set the cut to a predetermined depth. Although each requires slightly different techniques, you can make the same cuts with either of them. A plunge router offers more convenience, but at a higher cost.

If you're buying your first router, you won't go wrong with a good fixed-base machine. A fixed-base router will be substantially less expensive than a plunge router, but will do the same work for you. As your skills (and woodworker's dreams) increase, add a plunge router later.

COLLET SIZE

A router's collet size is comparable to a power drill's chuck size. The collet holds the shank of the bit and transmits the motor's power to it. Most collets are tightened by a wrench. Some routers' collets accept only ¼-inch shanks. Others are made to accept ½-inch shanks. Since the cutting head of the bit determines the size and shape of the cut, you might ask what difference the shank diameter makes. Router bits, particularly large ones that form complex contours, encounter severe side-load pressures as they rotate and are pushed into the wood. Thicker shanks resist such loads better. And they're more expensive. Bits with ¼-inch shanks are suitable for many router operations, so you can start with a router that has a ¼-inch collet. Later you may want to move up to a ½-inch router to tackle heavier work. You can install ¼-inch bits in a ½-inch

A ROUTER CAN...

■ Create molding patterns, decorative picture frames, and signs
■ Make raised-panel doors
■ Make dovetail and box joints
■ Shape edges
■ Cut internal designs
■ Cut grooves, dadoes, rabbets, mortise joints, and hinge mortises

router with an accessory collet. Most ½-inch routers come with the ¼-inch collet. Collets for ⅜-inch shanks are also available. There are no adapters for installing larger-shank bits in a ¼-inch router.

POWER AND WEIGHT

Routing requires precision; precision demands comfort and easy handling. You probably won't need an 18-pound, 3-hp professional plunge router for a starter tool, but a lightweight router with less than 1 hp may disappoint you with its inability to cut quickly and smoothly. A 1¼- to 1½-hp model (about 8 amps and 8 pounds) will handle just about everything you'll throw its way and you'll find its weight easy to control. If you intend to table-mount your router, go for one with 2 hp or more so it will be able to handle larger bits for joinery.

Pick up the tool before you buy it. Handle shape, heft, and balance vary widely, and you want to be comfortable when you use a router. Check the position of the power switch; make sure it's located within thumb or finger reach so you can snap the power off without fumbling around. A D-handle often has a trigger switch right under your index finger. A spindle lock and a flat top on the router make changing bits easier.

VARIABLE SPEEDS

Variable-speed control is a worthwhile feature for a router. Although power is important to keep the bit from bogging down, a router relies mainly on its speed for cutting. Higher speeds mean cleaner cuts. The optimum speed can vary among different cuts, however. Deep cuts or cuts with a large bit are often best done at a slower speed; light chamfering requires high speed.

Variable-speed routers all have electronic motor-speed control. You'll find speed-control knobs, graduated dials, and other speed-setting devices that adjust the router's speed continuously from about 8,000 to 24,000 rpm. Pick the one you find most convenient.

SPINDLE LOCKS AND OTHER FEATURES

A spindle lock is a feature worth looking for, and so is a dust port. A spindle lock is usually in the form of a button you press in to keep the spindle from turning. Changing and tightening a bit in the collet is easier with a spindle lock. Without one, you need to use two wrenches, one on the spindle and one

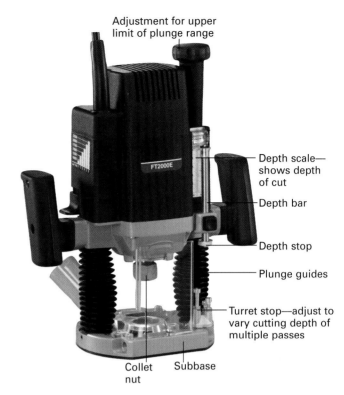

Adjustment for upper limit of plunge range

Depth scale—shows depth of cut

Depth bar

Depth stop

Plunge guides

Turret stop—adjust to vary cutting depth of multiple passes

Collet nut   Subbase

on the collet nut. A dust port allows you to connect the router to a dust-collection system or shop vac to pick up the chips as you work. This helps keep both your line of sight and your lungs clear of airborne particles.

Models with a soft-start feature minimize the sudden twist at start-up caused by the router's high torque. This useful feature makes handling the router easier, but does not increase the performance of the tool.

LAMINATE TRIMMER

Compact, lightweight, and slender, these high-speed units are designed for precision work, like trimming the edge on laminate kitchen countertops. Depth adjustment can be as fine as ¹⁄₁₂₈ inch with one-quarter turn of the knob. Most run at whining speeds (30,000 rpm), which can burn the work, so you must be careful with your feed speed. They will accept only ¼-inch bits—you won't need anything beefier for the work you'll be doing with this tool. Some manufacturers make larger trimmers that will also handle light-duty edge-routing normally reserved for a full-size router.

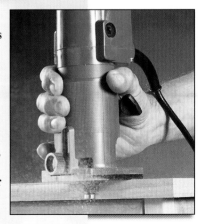

ROUTER
continued

Piloted bit—bearing rides on edge to keep cut consistent

Nonpiloted bit—requires a guide clamped to the work or commercial guide attached to the router

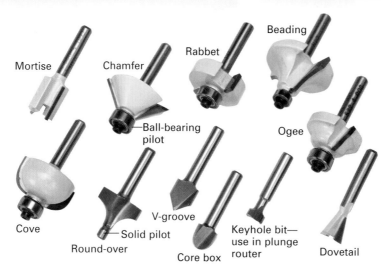

Mortise
Chamfer
Rabbet
Beading
Ball-bearing pilot
Ogee
Cove
V-groove
Round-over
Solid pilot
Core box
Keyhole bit—use in plunge router
Dovetail

COSTS

Router prices start at less than $100 for a tool suitable for occasional use. But once you've bought a router for one project, you'll probably just keep on finding uses for it. So, you should look at tools in the $150 range. There you should be able to find a fixed-base router with $1\frac{1}{4}$ or $1\frac{1}{2}$ hp. About $20 more will buy a basic plunge router. If you want a machine with lots of features, expect to pay $200 or more for either style.

ROUTER BITS

Bits are the key to a router's versatility. The variety of router bits available can seem confusing, but you'll make most of your cuts with about a dozen bits.

Router bits fall into two categories—edge cutters and field cutters. Edge-cutting bits finish the edges of your work in decorative profiles. The others cut the surface of the stock—forming grooves, veins, and hollows. Some commonly used bits are shown above left. Different sizes of each are available.

Pilot tips for edge bits make cutting easy—they maintain a set cutting depth without requiring a guide board clamped to the work or a guide on the router. A ball-bearing pilot is less likely to burn the workpiece than a solid one.

Carbide-tipped bits last longer than the less expensive high-speed steel ones, but they chip

Remove the base plate and with one wrench on the shaft, loosen the collet with another. Pull out the bit, clean the collet, insert another bit completely, and raise it about $\frac{1}{16}$ inch before tightening it.

To adjust the cutting depth for a fixed-base unit, loosen the base clamp and rotate either the adjustment ring or the motor (depending on the unit) until the bit depth is correct. Tighten the base clamp.

Base clamp

When adjusting a plunge router, place the shortest stop screw under the stop bar. Loosen the depth-stop clamp and seat the bar on the screw. With the plunge lock loosened, push the motor down until the bit touches the work. Tighten the knob and raise the stop bar until it clears the turret screw by the depth you want. Tighten the depth stop and loosen the plunge lock.

Stop bar

Turret stop

ROUTER SAFETY

Take these precautions when using a router.
■ Router bits work safest when they're clean and sharp. Inspect them regularly and keep them sharp.
■ Wear safety goggles/glasses and ear protection.
■ Unplug the tool before changing a bit.
■ Securing the work is mandatory with a router—this is a two-handed tool.
■ Turn power off after cutting; let the bit stop spinning before setting the router down.
■ Let bits cool after cutting.

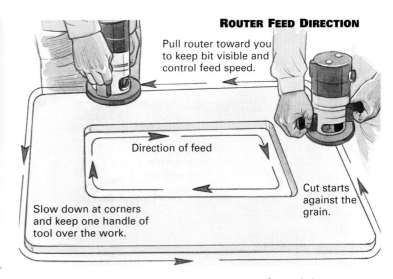

ROUTER FEED DIRECTION

Pull router toward you to keep bit visible and control feed speed.

Direction of feed

Slow down at corners and keep one handle of tool over the work.

Cut starts against the grain.

EDGE ROUTING
WITH PILOTED BIT

Pull router toward you.

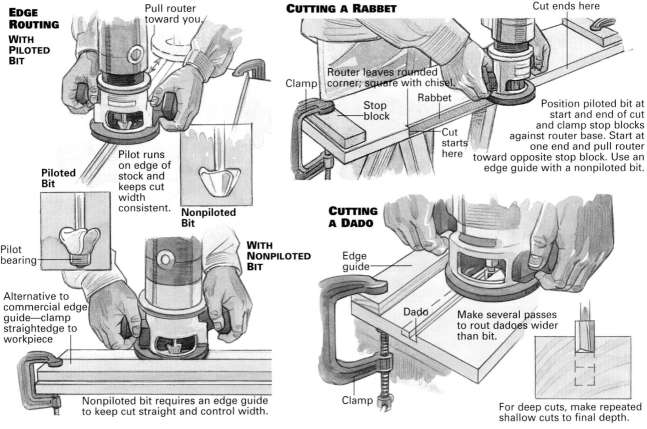

Pilot runs on edge of stock and keeps cut width consistent.

Piloted Bit

Nonpiloted Bit

Pilot bearing

WITH NONPILOTED BIT

Alternative to commercial edge guide—clamp straightedge to workpiece

Nonpiloted bit requires an edge guide to keep cut straight and control width.

CUTTING A RABBET

Cut ends here

Router leaves rounded corner; square with chisel.

Clamp

Rabbet

Stop block

Cut starts here

Position piloted bit at start and end of cut and clamp stop blocks against router base. Start at one end and pull router toward opposite stop block. Use an edge guide with a nonpiloted bit.

CUTTING A DADO

Edge guide

Dado

Make several passes to rout dadoes wider than bit.

Clamp

For deep cuts, make repeated shallow cuts to final depth.

ROUTING A CIRCLE

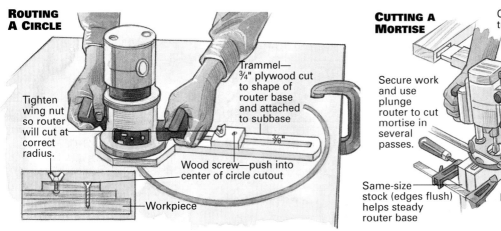

Tighten wing nut so router will cut at correct radius.

Trammel—¾" plywood cut to shape of router base and attached to subbase

3⁄8"

Wood screw—push into center of circle cutout

Workpiece

CUTTING A MORTISE

Cut tenon with table saw and transfer its outline to workpiece.

Plunge router

Secure work and use plunge router to cut mortise in several passes.

Use edge guide

Same-size stock (edges flush) helps steady router base

Mortise bit

Square ends with a chisel, bevel facing mortise.

ROUTER

continued

Mounting plate

Router sub-base attaches to bottom of mounting plate.

The router attaches to a separate mounting plate for most router tables. The plate then drops into the tabletop, as shown right.

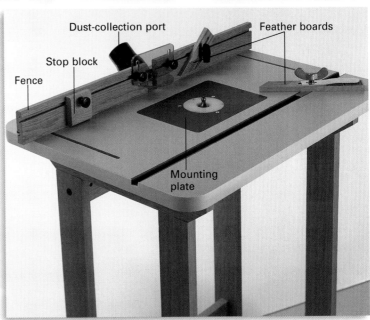

Dust-collection port

Feather boards

Stop block

Fence

Mounting plate

easily and won't stand up to being knocked around in a drawer. Stand your bits in a wood block so their edges don't touch.

USING A ROUTER

Some basic router cuts, techniques, and accessories are shown on page 39. Following the three recommendations below will ensure success in all router operations.

■ **SET CUTTING DEPTH AND LOCK IT:** When making a deep cut or removing a lot of material, start with a shallow cut. Finish the job with two or three progressively deeper cuts.

■ **CLAMP THE WORKPIECE SECURELY:** Make sure your workpiece won't move when you push the router into it. Set the router base on the workpiece, with the bit clear of the surface. Then start the router, let it spin up to full speed, and ease the bit into the stock.

■ **ROUT THE END GRAIN FIRST:** When routing all four edges of a piece, rout across the ends first. This way, any tearout will be cut away when you rout the edges. Always cut with the grain on the edges. Whenever possible, stand so you can move the router from left to right and opposite the bit rotation. Cutting in the direction of bit rotation—*climb cutting*—requires extra care to maintain control.

TABLE-MOUNTED ROUTERS

It's easier and safer to rout small workpieces with a router table. A table-mounted router also lets you make specialty joints and other cuts that are not practical with a handheld tool. Table-mounting a router is usually a matter of removing its base plate and attaching the router to a mounting plate that fits the table. (See the photos above.)

When you buy a commercial router table the router is not included. Most standard routers will fit most brands of tables, but you should ask the dealer to make sure your router will fit the table you want. Router tables span the range from small benchtop router stands to elaborate cabinets. There are even tables without legs so you can custom-build your own. Some table-saw extensions are designed to hold a router. They serve as a normal table extension when the router is not installed.

Common features on commercial tables include a split fence with independently

Mount a router in a table-saw extension to save shop space. Many table-saw manufacturers offer table extension wings designed to hold a router.

ROUTING EDGES

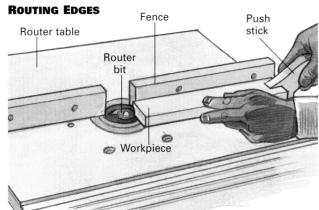

Turn router on and feed work slowly into cutter, keeping work flat against fence and table.

USING A MITER GAUGE

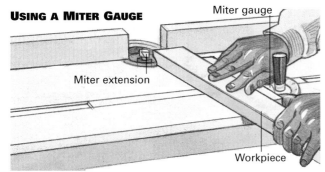

Set miter gauge at correct angle and feed work into cutter, holding work firmly on miter gauge.

MAKING STOPPED CUTS

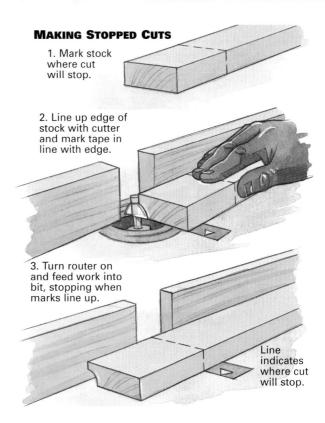

1. Mark stock where cut will stop.

2. Line up edge of stock with cutter and mark tape in line with edge.

3. Turn router on and feed work into bit, stopping when marks line up.

Line indicates where cut will stop.

adjustable sides, a bit guard, a groove for a miter gauge, and a dust-collection port. These make the table more convenient to use, but you can make accurate cuts on any table by clamping a fence or other guides to the table. Don't try to rout freehand unless the bit has a pilot bearing—you can't control the depth of cut and the bit could grab the workpiece, damaging it and possibly injuring you.

Many of the bits used for handheld routing will work fine in a table-mounted router. Some specialty bits are designated for table use only. They are generally larger bits, sometimes in matching sets, and require a ½-inch collet.

ROUTER-TABLE TIPS

A router table is great for trimming work to a template. When cutting to a template with a table router, attach the template to the work so the bit's pilot bearing rides against the edge of the template.

You can use your router table as a jointer for thin stock. Use a straight bit, and set the cutting depth with the infeed fence. Put the outfeed fence out slightly from the plane of the infeed fence to support the planed edge after it passes the bit.

SHAPER

A shaper is much like a table-mounted router built for continuous, heavy use. It's larger and more powerful than a router, but does similar work.

What distinguishes most shapers from router tables, aside from their power, table amenities, and size, are the cutters and the manner in which they are mounted. Shaper cutters mount on a threaded spindle and are secured in place with a nut, unlike router bits, which fit into a collet.

Although some shaper cutters are solid and form only one profile, molding heads with interchangeable knives and combination cutters will produce a variety of shapes. Combination cutters have several knives, which can be arranged in different order on the spindle to produce various profiles. Interchangeable cutting knives also help keep costs down—shaper cutters are often more expensive than router bits.

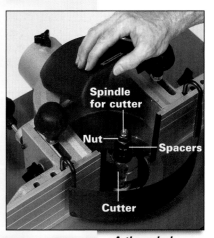

A threaded spindle holds the shaper cutter. Combination cutters and cutters with interchangeable knives can make a variety of shapes. The curved shield in front of the cutter slides up to clear the workpiece.

BISCUIT JOINER

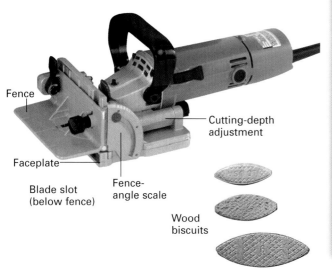

Fence

Cutting-depth adjustment

Faceplate

Blade slot (below fence)

Fence-angle scale

Wood biscuits

A biscuit joiner (sometimes called a plate joiner) does only one job, but no other tool makes joints as quickly and easily. Biscuit joiners cut crescent-shaped slots in both of the surfaces to be joined—football-shape wafers glued in the slots hold the joint together. Biscuit joints aren't as strong as dovetail or mortise-and-tenon joints, but they are as strong as or stronger than doweled joints. They're great for shelves, tabletops, and trim work and are effective for face frames and frames for cabinet doors. Biscuit joints are virtually foolproof. You don't have to worry about precision sawing and chiseling for dovetails, right-on-the-money drilling for dowels, or fine slicing for splines. Even if your slots are a little off the mark, you can adjust the joint side to side by about ⅛ inch for perfect alignment.

A BISCUIT JOINER CAN...

■ Cut slots for football-shaped disks that reinforce glue joints in wood

BUYING A BISCUIT JOINER

When shopping for a biscuit joiner, base your decision on the best combination of the following factors.

If you will be making mostly picture frames, shadow boxes, or lightweight cabinetry, a small joiner (4 pounds, 4 amps) will work fine (about $50). A joiner to make standard-size slots will cost a little more. One that is adjustable for biscuit sizes and has a motor of 5–7 amps (the power you'll need if you're making many joints in hardwood) will cost between $130 and $270.

Get the one that will handle the range of biscuit sizes you will most likely use. A machine with ball bearings will last longer and give you more accurate cuts than one with bushings. Make sure the handle is comfortable for you. Adjustable handles make

Lay out the joints and mark the center on each part, then cut the biscuit slots by aligning the center mark on the joiner with the mark on the joint.

CHANGING A BLADE

Unplug your biscuit joiner. If it has a blade guard, undo its retaining screws and remove the guard. Wearing leather gloves, slip the open-end wrench supplied with the tool under the blade so it holds the inner clamp washer. Then with the pin wrench, loosen the outer washer and remove it and the blade. Install the new blade, tighten the outer washer, and replace the blade guard.

JOINING EDGES—MARKING THE WORK AND CUTTING SLOTS

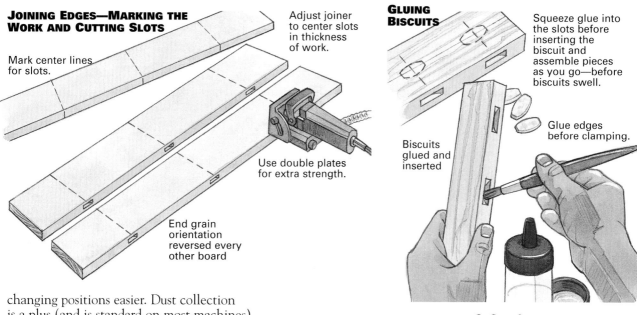

Mark center lines for slots.

Adjust joiner to center slots in thickness of work.

Use double plates for extra strength.

End grain orientation reversed every other board

changing positions easier. Dust collection is a plus (and is standard on most machines).

The fence and faceplate should be solid and have positive stops at 0, 45, and 90 degrees. All adjustments should move smoothly throughout their range and should be easy to lock securely.

BISCUITS

Cooking up sturdy joints with these funny-looking wafers means choosing biscuits to match the job.
- **WOOD:** Compressed-wood biscuits come in three standard sizes: 0 ($1\frac{3}{4}\times\frac{5}{8}$ inch), 10 ($2\frac{1}{8}\times\frac{3}{4}$ inch), and 20 ($2\frac{3}{8}\times1$ inch). All are $\frac{5}{32}$ inch thick. Birch or beechwood take glue better than other woods and swell consistently to make stout joints.
- **POLYPROPYLENE:** These UV-resistant biscuits are good for decks and outside work.
- **CLAMPING BISCUITS:** The patterned surface of these plastic biscuits grabs wood without glue for use in hard-to-clamp joints.
- **HARDWARE:** Fasteners to make knockdown furniture and light-duty hinges are some available hardware items that fit into biscuit-joiner slots.

BISCUIT JOINER SAFETY

- Keep blades clean and sharp.
- Always wear safety glasses or goggles.
- Unplug the joiner when changing a blade.
- Clamp workpiece, especially when cutting joints in end grain or mitered edges.
- Wear gloves when changing the blade.

GLUING BISCUITS

Squeeze glue into the slots before inserting the biscuit and assemble pieces as you go—before biscuits swell.

Glue edges before clamping.

Biscuits glued and inserted

CLAMPING JOINTS

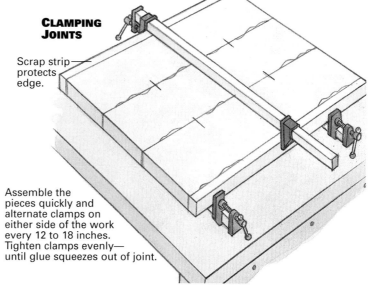

Scrap strip protects edge.

Assemble the pieces quickly and alternate clamps on either side of the work every 12 to 18 inches. Tighten clamps evenly—until glue squeezes out of joint.

EDGE-TO-FACE JOINERY

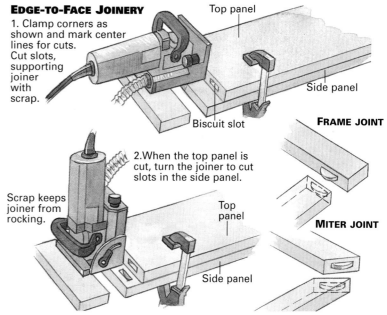

1. Clamp corners as shown and mark center lines for cuts. Cut slots, supporting joiner with scrap.

Top panel

Side panel

Biscuit slot

2. When the top panel is cut, turn the joiner to cut slots in the side panel.

Scrap keeps joiner from rocking.

Top panel

Side panel

FRAME JOINT

MITER JOINT

POWER PLANER

12,000 to more than 20,000 rpm. It turns counterclockwise (looking from the right side of the tool). Cutting depth adjusts by raising or lowering the front sole plate, usually with a knob. Raising the front plate deepens the cut. The rear plate is fixed; it rides on the surface that has just been planed.

Power planers perform many of the same feats as belt sanders, but they do them more quickly and smoothly. Midsize models (3¼ inches wide) are perfect for fitting doors, cabinetmaking, and even for leveling crowned floor joists or bowed studs so the finished surface lies flat. Most do-it-yourselfers won't need a larger plane—they're available up to 6⅛ inches wide. You can simply make several passes when you need to plane surfaces wider than the 3¼-inch planer.

Most planers have two blades in a cutterhead that's as wide as the tool's base plate. The cutterhead spins at anywhere from

BUYING A PLANER

Home-use power planers have about 3- to 7-amp motors. For occasional DIY use, 4-amp models are available for less than $100. But if you will use your planer frequently or for heavy work, you should probably look for one with at least a 6-amp motor, priced in the $150 range. Power planers aimed at professional woodworkers cost $250 or more. They have motors of at least 7 amps, ravenous cutting capacity, and butter-smooth adjustments.

USING YOUR POWER PLANER

Power planers can chew through wood faster than you can blink, so machine control is of the utmost importance.
■ Plan to reach your final cutting depth in several passes. By taking shallower cuts, your cuts will be more accurate, and you won't bog down the motor.
■ Always turn the power on before you bring the blades in contact with the work.
■ With both hands on the planer, place the front shoe on the work and apply pressure on the front of the planer. As the blade begins to cut, equalize the pressure on both ends and keep it consistent along the entire length of the workpiece until you approach the end. Keep your forward motion consistent. Above all, don't rush the tool.

PLANING WITH THE GRAIN

Depth control moves front sole up or down to adjust cutting depth.

Move planer in direction of grain.

Feed direction

Front sole

Direction of blade rotation

Rear sole (fixed)

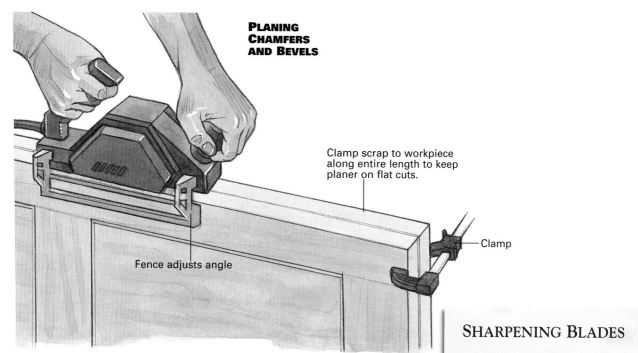

PLANING CHAMFERS AND BEVELS

Clamp scrap to workpiece along entire length to keep planer on flat cuts.

Clamp

Fence adjusts angle

SHARPENING BLADES

Planer blades get dull after 4 to 5 hours of work—quicker if you're removing paint. You'll know when it's time to sharpen when the motor works harder, your stock gets burned, or the tool produces sawdust instead of chips.

Cutterheads vary among power planers; some have removable blades. Blades must be sharpened precisely to maintain the planer's accuracy, so you may want to leave sharpening to a professional. When you reinstall the blades, they must be positioned to cut flush with the surface of the rear sole.

■ When you approach the end of the work, let up slightly on the rear plate pressure and slow your forward motion.

■ Adjust the forward speed to the material you're planing. In woods that cut more easily, you can feed the tool a little faster.

■ If the edge is bumpy or uneven, mark the high spots with a pencil and plane them close to level before planing the entire edge.

■ Whenever possible, cut with the grain, not against it. (See the illustration on the opposite page.)

■ Start planing a taper in the thickest part of the stock. Begin with short strokes, then lengthen the successive passes.

POWER PLANER SAFETY

■ Make sure the cord is out of the way of blades—throw it over your shoulder.
■ Always wear safety glasses/goggles and ear protection.
■ Make sure workpiece is clean and free of metal.
■ Keep fingers away from spinning blade.

PLANING END GRAIN

To avoid tearing out edges when planing an end, plane each end to about ⅔ of the width of the work.

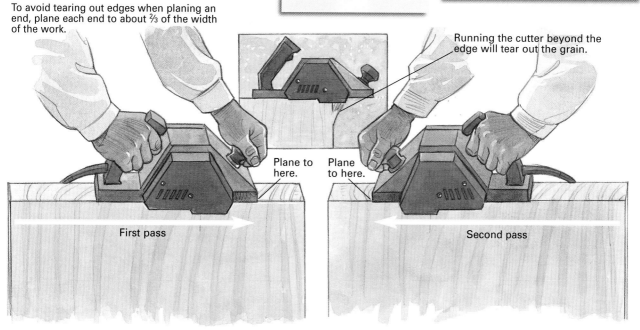

Running the cutter beyond the edge will tear out the grain.

Plane to here.

Plane to here.

First pass

Second pass

ROTARY HAND TOOL

A ROTARY HAND TOOL CAN...

■ Perform almost any task done by other power tools—in miniature
■ Cut, grind, drill, polish, sharpen, rout, sand, and finish materials for hobbies, models, and other fine craftwork

Rotary tools are often sold in kits with bits, sanders, grinders, and other accessories to adapt the tool to many uses. This one includes a flexible shaft.

With speeds up to 30,000 rpm and the capability to spin a variety of bits—from twist drills to polishing pads—rotary hand tools are the whiz kids of the home workshop. They can do just about anything larger tools can do, only in miniature. That makes them perfect not only for hobbies and crafts, but also for other kinds of detail work—furniture refinishing, polishing jewelry and other fine objects, drilling in tight spots, cutting small stock, and so many other tasks that you might not know where to start using it. Mounted in a stand and equipped with a flexible shaft, a rotary tool lets you bring finesse to your work that would be impossible with any other tool.

ROTARY TOOL SAFETY

Don't be lulled into unsafe habits by the small size of rotary hand tools and their cutters and abrasives. Anything that will shape wood or plastic can cut you and surrounding surfaces.
■ If your tool is equipped with a power lock switch, make sure to disengage it and let the tool stop spinning before resting it on the worktable.
■ Wear eye protection—safety glasses or goggles. These tools can spit chips and particles.
■ Maintain a firm grip on the tool and don't use so much pressure that you risk having the bit slip and damage another surface.

BUYING A ROTARY HAND TOOL

For all their versatility, rotary hand tools might surprise you with their low price. You can buy an engraver without accessories for less than $20 and a high-quality variable-speed tool (again, without bits) for a little more than twice that. Add accessories in a kit, and the price tag comes to about $70; with a flexible shaft, about $80. More powerful flexible-shaft machines cost more. Handpieces for these machines can take larger tool shanks, suiting them to heavier work.

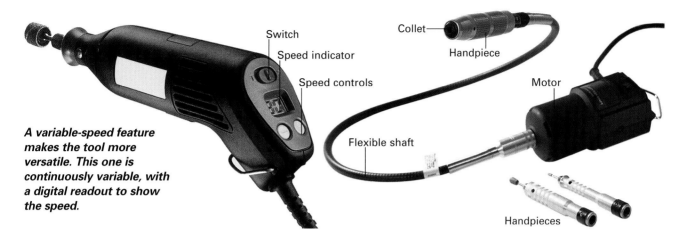

Switch
Speed indicator
Speed controls
Collet
Handpiece
Motor
Flexible shaft
Handpieces

A variable-speed feature makes the tool more versatile. This one is continuously variable, with a digital readout to show the speed.

How do you decide what accessories you need? Since many models come packaged as kits with a wide assortment of accessories, making your initial choices will not prove difficult—the manufacturer has already done it for you. Buy the minimum assortment you think you'll need, then add other items later as you need them for your projects.

CUTTING BITS AND OTHER ACCESSORIES

Bits for rotary hand tools come as mounted or unmounted. A mounted cutter is permanently affixed to its shank, so when it's too worn for use, you throw it away and get a new one. Unmounted tools attach to a mandrel, a shaft with one end capable of accepting a screw or nut-and-bolt assembly that holds the tool to it. When the tool is worn, its replacement mounts on the mandrel. Saws and sanding and buffing tools usually mount on a mandrel.

When you buy new or replacement tips, be sure you know the range of shank sizes your model will accept. Most ⅛-inch collets and chucks will take a minimum shaft diameter of ³⁄₃₂ inch. A typical ¹⁄₁₆-inch tool will accommodate shafts down to ¹⁄₆₄ inch. If you need something smaller than the range of your tool, you can purchase an adapter chuck that will hold tiny shafts, such as wire-gauge drills.

With accessory bases and stands, the tool becomes a router, a drill press, a grinder, or other tools.
■ **CUTTING:** With rotary hand tool cutting tips, you have two choices. Use saws for wood, soft metals, and plastics. Abrasive cutoff

WORKING WITH PLASTICS

Working with certain plastics demands a light touch. Thermoplastic materials such as acrylic and plexiglass will soften or melt if the tool generates too much heat. To keep their edges—and your sanding drum or cutting wheel—clean, apply pressure lightly and remove the tip from the work frequently.

Fluted cutters and coarse abrasives will not clog up as quickly as finer tools or abrasives. If things do get gummed up, let the wheel cool down. That will allow the plastic to reharden, and you can remove it with a stiff brush.

Hard plastics of the thermosetting kind won't soften. You can work them pretty much as you would work wood.

A flexible-shaft machine with a larger separate motor offers more power than a handheld rotary tool. Handpieces can accept tool shanks up to ¼ inch.

Keep your tools clean and rust-free with a wire brush and a rotary tool.

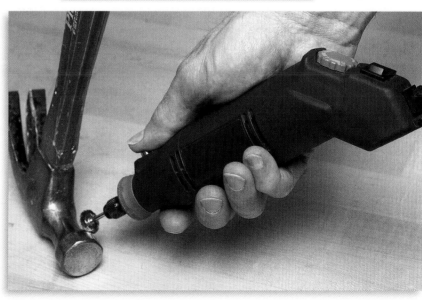

ROTARY HAND TOOL
continued

The rotary tool is perfect for shaping, carving, and sculpting.

A rotary tool engraves your property for identification.

You can remove tile grout with this accessory.

A right-angle attachment helps reach into tight spots.

Cut holes in walls (above) or trim tile (below) with this accessory.

wheels are made for ferrous or nonferrous metals.

■ **SHARPENING:** With the right aluminum oxide tip on a rotary hand tool, you can expand the definition of the word "sharpening." You can clean out the teeth on your table-saw blade with one shape, sharpen your chain saw with another, true the edge of small tools with still another. Touch-up sharpening of large tools is well within the reach of these tips. Renewing the edge of a chisel or ax blade is best done on a bench grinder. When sharpening, mount the tool in a bench stand.

■ **ENGRAVING:** Many homeowner insurance carriers recommend engraving your name in all household objects of value. This tool is about the only one you can use for this purpose. Use a small engraving tip and take a trial run on scrap metal. Hold the tip perpendicular to the object to keep it from wandering.

■ **DRILLING:** If you've ever tried to predrill for a curtain rod next to an adjacent wall, you know that a portable drill won't fit. Bring out a rotary tool and you'll be done in seconds. It will give you access when drilling in other tight spots, such as drilling holes for handles in a narrow drawer. Use a slow speed. A drill press stand lets you drill precisely and accurately with small drill bits.

■ **GRINDING:** Grinding tips and wheels come in many shapes, sizes, and abrasive grades. In addition to their sharpening uses, you can take burrs off tubing with them, enlarge holes in metal or ceramic tile so you can make a bolt or plumbing fixture fit, and even smooth out minor chips in glass.

■ **POLISHING:** Steel and brass wire brushes will clean rust off small metal objects quickly. Softer brushes, nylon and natural bristle, will clean up soft materials. Put a dab of polishing compound on a buffing wheel to polish rings and other small objects. Use low speeds and light pressure when polishing to avoid either melting or burnishing the surface.

TOOL TIPS

For rotary tool tasks, let the speed of the tool do the work. With the bit spinning at up to 30,000 rpm, you won't need anything but light pressure to do most jobs. A hot tool or a sudden drop in speed is a sure sign you're forcing the work.

Large, heavy pieces will probably let you work freehand without clamping them. When working freehand, keep control of the unit so it won't wander off the contours of your design.

Put small pieces in a clamp or vise, or when that's impractical, fasten the tool in a stand, hold the work with one hand and use a flexible shaft in the other. In all cases, keep your hands out of the line of the tip. Rotary hand tools can slip and cause serious injury.

NAILERS AND STAPLERS

An electric nailer or stapler is like having a third hand—these tools let you hold the pieces of the work in place with one hand and fasten it accurately with the other.

Of course, you can use a spring-loaded fastener or hammer stapler for many of the chores electric fastening tools will do, but spring-loaded and hammer tools quickly tire your hand and jam easily. And it's not always easy to swing a hammer stapler or tacker accurately.

There aren't as many models of electric nailers or staplers available as there are air-powered ones, but there's a sufficient variety on the market to meet most household needs. Air-powered tools require an air compressor and can take more time to set up. With an electric fastener, you just load it, plug it in, and go to work. Electric brad nailers are better suited to working with softwood; if you have a lot of hardwood assembly to do, air-power tools are better. Likewise, if you want a nailer that will drive large nails for framing or other heavy work, air- or gas-powered tools are your only choices.

With the electric nailer or stapler you can glue up joints without clamping them—just pop a couple of brads or staples into the joint while the glue sets. The tools make cabinet assembly quick and easy. Use a nailer or stapler to assemble picture frames, hang paneling, install baseboards and chair rails, install window and door trim, tack up insulation and vapor barrier, and fasten tackless strip and carpet.

CHOOSING A FASTENER

A 10-amp electric nailer will do most of your jobs without complaint. It should be able to drive 18-gauge steel brads from ⅝ to 1 inch long. These brads have plenty of holding power but are less likely to split the wood. More power lets you use longer brads, up to 1¼ inches with 14 amps. About $50 will buy a 10-amp nailer. Expect to pay more than $100 for a 14-amp model.

NAILERS AND STAPLERS CAN...

■ Quickly, and with little effort on your part, fasten trim, carpet, ceiling tile, insulation, and other materials

Safety lock

Trigger

Magazine

This electric nailer takes brads up to 1¼ inches long. Some tools shoot both brads and staples, suiting them to a variety of fastening chores. A power nailer or stapler is especially handy in situations like the ceiling installation shown below.

Stapler prices vary as well, but expect costs in a higher range. Be sure to do a little research on what size staples you are likely to need. First there's *crown size*, the width of the staple—generally ³⁄₁₆, ⅜, or ½ inch. Smaller staples work for light assembly, wider ones for heavier work like carpet and cabinets. Staple length (from ⅛ to ⁹⁄₁₆ inch) is a function of how thick your work is. Any fastener should penetrate the stock by at least two-thirds of its length.

For between $120 and $140, you can purchase a stapler that will drive five lengths of narrow crown (³⁄₁₆ inch) staples. Driving wider crown staples costs more—$185 to $195, with the same multilength capability. When using either tool, make sure to press its nose against the work before you squeeze the trigger. If you don't, the tool will pop away from the work, leaving you with a fastener sticking out of the surface that you'll have to pull out.

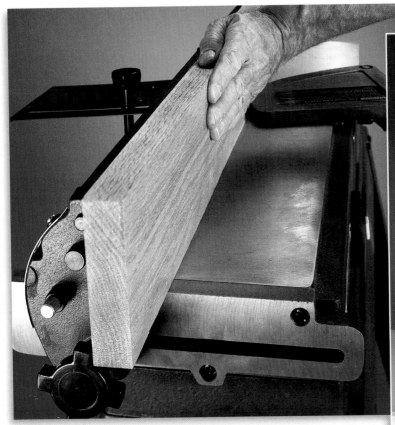

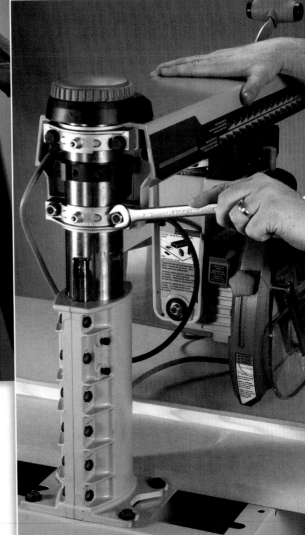

STATIONARY AND BENCHTOP TOOLS

Stationary and benchtop tools are the kings of the power-tool world. Some of them perform the same tasks as their handheld counterparts, but they do them faster and more accurately. Others are designed to do things no other tool will do.

You can drill holes with a portable drill, for example, but drilling precisely spaced holes for adjustable shelving along both sides of a home-built bookcase goes much faster on a drill press. You can cut dimensioned framing lumber to size with a portable circular saw, but a miter saw will do it faster—and it will cut accurate joints for picture frames too. When it comes to shearing thin stock from a 6-inch piece of rough timber or shaping the curved outline of a decorative table, you need a band saw. But a band-saw blade isn't fine enough to produce delicate fretwork, nor can it make inside cutouts with just a small hole for a starting point. That's where your scroll saw comes in.

You probably don't need every tool described in this chapter—at least not right away. It's wise to start out with the tools that meet your most immediate needs, then buy additional ones as your skill and interest (and budget) are ready for them.

Start with a list of your upcoming projects. Then review the sections in this chapter devoted to the tools that will help with them. Read woodworking publications for tool reviews and drop in on a few users' forums on the Internet or go to some of the manufacturers' and suppliers' websites. Then get catalogs and visit your local distributors. These steps will put you well on your way to setting up your own customized workshop.

From table saws to jointers, thickness planers to shapers, drill presses to lathes, stationary power tools have the muscle to help you complete a variety of woodworking projects with ease, precision, and safety. Many of them will perform multiple tasks. Analyze your woodworking or home maintenance needs and buy the tools that will provide you with the most versatility.

TABLE SAW

A 10-inch contractor's table saw offers plenty of power and precision. An accessory mobile base makes the saw easy to position for use in a cramped shop.

The table saw is the centerpiece of many workshops. It rips, crosscuts, miter-cuts, bevel-cuts, dadoes, rabbets, tapers, and trims—all with precision and speed unmatched by any other tool.

Table saws come in three styles—benchtop saws, contractor's saws, and cabinet saws.

BENCHTOP TABLE SAW

Benchtop saws are the smallest and least expensive of the group, but they can do serious work. Many woodworkers start out with a benchtop saw and produce furniture and home renovations aplenty before shop space and budgets allow a larger saw.

Benchtop saws save on size and weight by driving the blade directly with a universal motor and by using aluminum and synthetic materials instead of cast iron or steel. Weight loss does not come without sacrifices, however. These saws are noisy when they're working, and the lighter construction doesn't absorb vibration, which transfers to the entire unit and can make consistent accurate cuts more difficult to achieve. Look for a saw with the motor mounted on two cast-aluminum brackets; these mountings don't flex as easily and reduce vibration somewhat more than pin-mounted motors.

Motors are usually in the 15-amp range; in most saws that's power enough to cut through 2-inch stock. Buy the saw with the deepest right-angle and beveled depth you can afford. An electric brake, which stops the blade from spinning when you turn the power off, is a worthwhile safety feature.

Most benchtop table saws are ribbed, but smooth tops are available. A smooth top might make sawing easier for some users. Many benchtop models have maximum rip capacity of 24 inches (the distance from the fence to the blade), and there are a few on the market with larger capacity.

Pay close attention to the fence and miter gauge on benchtop saws—precision in these parts is valuable. A fence that locks into place with lock-down levers is easier to set accurately than a fence that slides into place and locks with screw-down knobs at front and back. The miter gauge should slide smoothly in the slots without play.

As a last test, run the blade-tilt and blade-height adjustments through their motions. Look for smooth operation. Some models tilt and raise with left-hand threads, some with right-hand threads. You can probably become accustomed to either one relatively quickly.

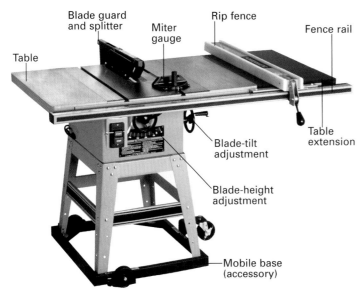

Table
Blade guard and splitter
Miter gauge
Rip fence
Fence rail
Blade-tilt adjustment
Blade-height adjustment
Table extension
Mobile base (accessory)

CONTRACTOR'S SAW

A contractor's saw is a step up from a benchtop saw—in both power and precision—and a small step down in portability. The larger, heavier contractor's saw stands on attached legs. That might be important if you're going to be moving the saw to a work site often. But for many, a table saw is a permanent fixture in a shop.

An important difference between a contractor's saw and a benchtop saw is how the blade is driven. The contractor's saw has an induction motor that drives the blade through a belt. The motor either hangs out the rear of the saw or is mounted inboard. (Inboard motors are usually quieter.) Induction motors run more quietly and smoothly than universal motors. Heavier cast-iron and steel parts dampen vibrations too.

Motors are usually 12- to 18-amp models. You need one of about 15 amps and 1½ to 2 hp. Check out the arbor and motor mountings also; heavier construction pays off in longer life and accuracy.

Up and down the price range, you'll find tables made of different materials, but cast-iron provides more stability than other materials. Be careful of the edges, though; cast-iron tables can have sharp edges. A table with a beveled front edge will minimize cut materials and fingers. Get as much open table space in front of the blade slot as you can—at least 11 inches. Tables with T-slots for the miter gauge bar retain the miter gauge through its full extension. The miter gauge may tip out of an open rectangular slot at the end of a long cut.

Table extensions increase the utility of the saw. Cast-iron extensions won't move much under the weight of wide and heavy stock, but cast aluminum will hold up well enough for most home-workshop use.

The rip fence is a crucial part of a table saw. First check the adjustment and lock-down mechanisms. Smooth movement and lock-down levers are preferable. Run the fence back and forth along the bars and lock it in place several times to make sure it operates smoothly, has no play when it's locked down, and stays parallel to the blade and square to the table every time. Take a tape measure along when you shop to check the fence.

With the fence locked, check its ability to resist side pressure. A fence that deflects when locked leads to sloppy cuts and can bind the work against the blade, causing kickback. If you find a saw that meets all your specifications except fence quality, you may be able to remedy the problem with an upgraded fence from the saw manufacturer or an aftermarket fence. Many dealers sell package deals comprising a contractor's saw and a high-quality aftermarket fence.

Small, lightweight, and less expensive, benchtop table saws are ideal where workshop space or budget is restricted. They aren't as powerful or accurate as contractor's or cabinet saws, however.

Try the blade-tilt and cutting-height controls—they should run their full range without binding. Controls placed well below the table are easier to get at and use, but more important is the number of revolutions it takes to run the blade full scale. Fewer revolutions per inch save time but can be less accurate. Controls with finesse, on the other hand, will take more setup time. You'll find 5-inch wheels require less energy to turn, no matter what their adjustment ratios are.

CABINET SAW

The cabinet saw is king of the table-saw world. Many cabinet saws have a smaller footprint than a contractor's saw, but saving space is not the usual reason for buying one.

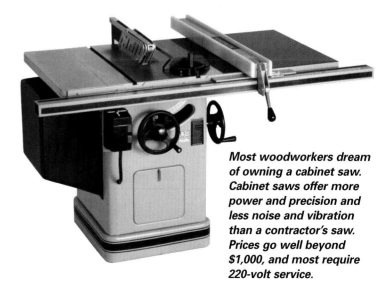

Most woodworkers dream of owning a cabinet saw. Cabinet saws offer more power and precision and less noise and vibration than a contractor's saw. Prices go well beyond $1,000, and most require 220-volt service.

TABLE SAW
continued

Always unplug the saw before changing a blade or making tune-up adjustments. To change a blade, remove the table insert and raise the blade to maximum height. Then immobilize it by pressing a piece of scrap wood against the teeth, and loosen the arbor nut. Set the new blade on the arbor and tighten the nut.

A cabinet saw is made to cut large stock all day with consistency, and everything about one (including its cost) is beefier. The sheer mass and weight of a cabinet saw (about 350 pounds minimum) results in lower vibration, less noise, and more accurate cuts, even in large and heavy workpieces. The motor is enclosed, and the saw base is closed, which makes dust collection more efficient.

Cabinet-saw motors start out at about 3 hp, roughly twice the power of the contractor's saws commonly in use. That power should be sufficient for cutting through material up to the maximum cutting depth of 3⅛ inches. Heavy-duty motors may be 5 hp or more. Most cabinet-saw motors draw enough current that they should be connected to a 220-volt circuit.

Increased power means fewer burned cuts—you can keep the work moving fast enough that the blade won't heat up any one area enough to burn it. Motor, drive belts, and arbor are all enclosed in the unit's base cabinet.

Cast-iron is the standard in cabinet-saw tables and table extensions. Thicker and better-finished castings are signs of a high-quality saw. There can be differences in finish, even on saws that cost this much. Mirror finishes are available, but not absolutely necessary. Many of the features that are optional on a contractor's saw are standard on most cabinet saws. These include T-slots for miter gauge bars, large and smooth-operating tilt and blade-height controls, and extra-large, easy-to-reach power switches—usually a magnetic switch. Larger table extensions are usually available for these big saws.

COSTS

Benchtop saws start at less than $150. Saws at the bottom of the price range are best suited to sizing rough stock. For about $190, you can get a table saw that is reasonably accurate for hobby and home-project work. At slightly over the $300 mark you'll find saws able to do heavier and more accurate work. Saws priced around $550 are higher-quality models with electronic speed controls (not essential for a table saw) and remarkably accurate fences.

Basic contractor's saws are available for between $200 and $300, but getting the level of quality, durability, power, control, smoothness, and accuracy that won't leave you disappointed will cost between $700 and $800. Those prices approach the lower end of the cabinet-saw price range, which goes beyond $3,000.

BLADES

Most table saws, including benchtop saws, use a 10-inch blade. Many saws come equipped with a steel combination blade, which will get you through most cuts but isn't necessarily the best choice for any of them. When you replace it, buy a carbide-tipped 40- to 50-tooth combination blade. Blade design and manufacturing technology now make combo blades suited to most cutting. Add a separate rip blade if you need it. Thin-kerf blades are good for benchtop saws; they take out less wood than a thicker blade and therefore don't work the motor as hard.

Changing the blade is similar for most table saws. Unplug the saw, then immobilize the blade. You can usually hold it by pressing a short length of scrapwood against the teeth. If it's too tight, grip the blade with a plastic blade holder that fits over the top of the blade, available from many tool dealers. Remove the arbor nut, then slip the blade and blade washers off the arbor. Place the washers and the new blade onto the arbor, then reinstall the arbor nut. Immobilize the blade as you did for removal while you tighten the nut with a wrench. Tighten the arbor nut securely.

SETTING UP AND TUNING YOUR TABLE SAW

Depending on the amount of assembly your saw requires, you may need to do some testing and tuning before you start using it. The steps and photos on the opposite page show some of the basic procedures. Refer to your saw's instruction manual for specific details. Unplug the saw before you make any adjustments.

■ **PARALLEL ALIGNMENT:** Table-saw blades must cut parallel to the miter-gauge slots and perpendicular (square) to the table surface. To check for parallel, raise the blade to its full height and measure the distance from the inside edge of the miter-gauge slot to both ends of the blade. For precision, measure to the same tooth by measuring at the front of the blade slot, then rotating the blade tooth to the back of the slot. If the measurements are the same, your blade is parallel. If the measurements are different, loosen the blade carriage bolts (under the table) and reposition the carriage. Measure again and tighten the bolts carefully when the blade is aligned correctly. Hold onto the carriage as you tighten the bolts.

■ **CHECKING FOR SQUARE:** Raise the blade to its full height and set the tilt scale to 0 degrees. Place one side of a square on the narrower side of the table, with its other leg touching the blade body between teeth. Turn the tilt control to remove any gap between the square and the blade, loosening the perpendicular stop screw if necessary. When the gap is gone, tighten the stop screw and readjust the pointer by loosening the lock screw or bending the pointer. Even when using a high-quality, well-maintained saw, it's wise to check the accuracy of any angle before you cut. An adjustable drafting triangle works well for this.

■ **SQUARING THE MITER GAUGE:** Once your blade is square to the table, set the miter gauge in the slot and lay a framing square with one leg on the blade and the other on the miter-gauge head. Loosen the locking handle and retighten it when the gauge is flush against the square. Reposition the miter gauge pointer, if necessary.

■ **SNUGGING THE MITER GAUGE:** If your miter gauge slips from side to side in the slot, dimple one edge of the bar with a metal punch. Stagger the dimples and make them only deep enough to keep the gauge in place. File them down slightly if the fit has become too tight.

■ **ADJUSTING THE RIP FENCE:** The rip fence must be nearly parallel to the blade— .015 inch farther from the blade line at the rear of the table than at the front. This keeps the stock from binding as it passes the blade. After making sure the blade is parallel to the miter-gauge slot, lower the blade all the way and slide the fence over so it's even with the front inside edge of the slot. Lock the fence. Loosen the bolts on the fence slightly, then place a piece of wood firmly against the front end of the fence. Run the miter gauge to the rear of the table and adjust the fence for .015 inch clearance. Use a feeler gauge or a fresh $1 bill. Tighten the bolts when the alignment is exact.

■ **ALIGNING THE SPLITTER:** Bend the splitter with hand screws until it is in line with the blade. If necessary, you can change the position of the blade guard by shimming it with washers on the mounting bolts.

CHECKING BLADE FOR SQUARE

SQUARING THE MITER GAUGE

SNUGGING THE MITER GAUGE

ADJUSTING THE RIP FENCE

ALIGNING THE SPLITTER

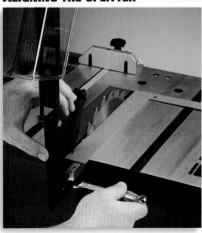

TABLE SAW
continued

MAKING CROSSCUTS

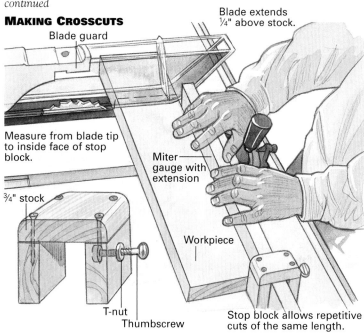

Blade guard

Blade extends ¼" above stock.

Measure from blade tip to inside face of stop block.

Miter gauge with extension

¾" stock

Workpiece

T-nut
Thumbscrew

Stop block allows repetitive cuts of the same length.

MAKING MITERS

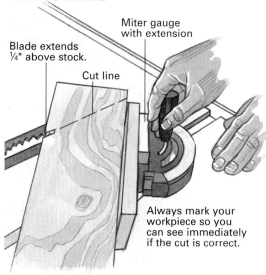

Miter gauge with extension

Blade extends ¼" above stock.

Cut line

Always mark your workpiece so you can see immediately if the cut is correct.

USING YOUR TABLE SAW

As the illustrations on these pages show, the techniques for making basic cuts on your table saw are not complicated. Two rules apply to all cuts—raise the blade no more than ¼ inch higher than the thickness of the stock and, whenever possible, stand to one side of the blade, not directly behind it. A few additional tips will help you increase the speed and accuracy of your work.

■ **BASIC CROSSCUTTING PROCEDURES:** To make crosscuts, mark the work at the desired length and place it with a true (straight) edge against the miter gauge. Standing behind the gauge, place your right hand on the miter gauge and hold the work against it with your left hand. Push the gauge with both hands slowly past the blade, then turn off the saw. When the blade stops spinning, return the miter gauge to the front of the table and remove the cutoff.

When crosscutting stock that extends off the front edge of the table, you can install the miter gauge backward. If the workpiece is longer or wider than the table and extensions, support it with extensions or outfeed rollers. (See the illustration on the opposite page.)

Always use the miter gauge when crosscutting and never press the end of a piece being crosscut against the rip fence—

STOPPING A CREEPING BLADE

If your table saw blade seems to creep back down into the table when you're cutting, try this. Set the cutting height by moving up to it, not down. Crank the blade below the height you want, then crank it up to the correct height and lock it securely. Disappearing blades are often caused by a slight play in the adjustment assemblies. Raising the blade keeps their parts in constant contact with each other.

TABLE-SAW SAFETY

Table saws will do almost anything you ask of them, but they're dangerous. Approach them with plenty of respect. Observe the following practices to avoid kickbacks and injuries.

■ Avoid cutting unseasoned or warped wood, which is more likely to bind in the blade and kickback.

■ Extend the blade a maximum of ¼ inch above the thickness of the work. More blade exposure means more exposure to risk.

■ Never remove the blade guard. Doing so removes at least three safety features—the splitter that helps keep the kerf open and the blade from binding, the housing itself, which keeps your fingers away from the blade and prevents chips from being propelled at you, and antikickback devices that reduce kickback on rip cuts.

■ On any cut narrower than 5 inches, use a push stick. It will help reduce kickback and keep your hands higher than the blade.

■ Outfeed rollers will keep you from reaching over the blade when cutting large stock. Use them to keep you from trying to catch the cut piece when it falls away from the table.

■ Wear ear and eye protection. Table saws are very noisy, and they propel chips and splinters at blinding speeds.

the cutoff will catch between the blade and the fence and be thrown back at you. To make a bevel cut, tilt the saw blade to the correct angle, and feed the work into the blade as for a crosscut.

You can fasten extensions to most miter gauges with screws or bolts. Extensions increase support for the workpiece, and by aligning your cut lines with the kerf through the extension, you can make repeated cuts to a predetermined length. Stop blocks are also handy for repeat cuts. (See the illustration on the opposite page.)

■ **BASIC RIP-CUTTING TECHNIQUES:** If the stock is longer than the table, set up outfeed supports. Then set the width of the cut on the rip guide and lock the fence in place. When precision matters, double-check the adjustment by measuring from the inside edge of the fence to the inside point of a tooth at both the front and rear of the blade.

Place the board flat on the table and snug it against the front end of the fence. Push the work into the fence with your left hand, keeping it as far away from the blade as possible and always at the front of the table ahead of the blade. Feed the workpiece steadily into the blade with your right hand and a push stick, as shown above right.

Always use the fence when making rip cuts. Push sticks should always be thinner than the width of the cut you're making. You can buy commercial sticks or make your own from plywood. Don't use solid stock, which can break along the grain.

■ **CUTTING MITERS:** Determine the angle of the cut by dividing 360 degrees by twice the number of sides of the finished piece. (The joints of a four-sided picture frame are cut at 45 degrees, an octagon at 22½ degrees.) Always mark the angle on the workpiece—the line will give you instant reference to gauge the accuracy of the cut. Set the miter gauge at the correct angle. The blade will tend to pull the workpiece along the edge of the miter gauge because it is going through the grain at an angle. The work will also tend to pivot on the trailing edge of the gauge. To alleviate these problems, use a miter-gauge extension with a slightly rough surface. You can clamp the work to the extension for extra security. To cut a compound miter—an angle and a bevel combined—tilt the saw blade to the bevel angle and set the miter gauge to the miter angle. Compound miters require a sharp blade. Test-cut a piece of scrapwood before cutting the finished work.

MAKING RIP CUTS WITH A TABLE SAW

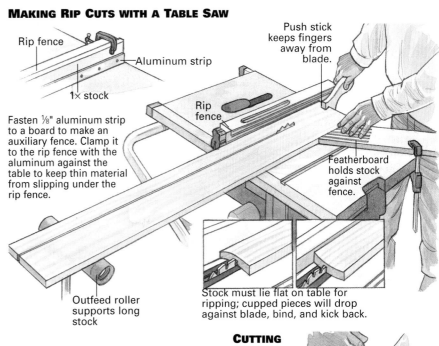

Rip fence

Aluminum strip

1× stock

Fasten ⅛" aluminum strip to a board to make an auxiliary fence. Clamp it to the rip fence with the aluminum against the table to keep thin material from slipping under the rip fence.

Push stick keeps fingers away from blade.

Rip fence

Featherboard holds stock against fence.

Outfeed roller supports long stock

Stock must lie flat on table for ripping; cupped pieces will drop against blade, bind, and kick back.

■ **CUTTING OVERSIZE SHEETS:** Sheet goods such as plywood can be difficult to handle on a table saw. Minimize the strain on the workpiece (and the operator) by providing plenty of support on the edge that extends beyond the table. Clamping a cleat perpendicular to the underside of the workpiece will help keep the cuts straight. (See the illustration below.)

CUTTING LARGE SHEETS ON A TABLE SAW

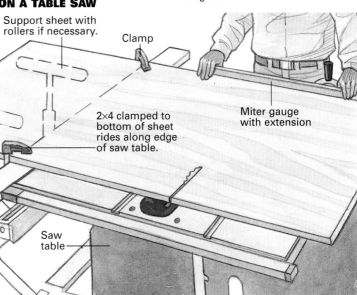

Support sheet with rollers if necessary.

Clamp

2×4 clamped to bottom of sheet rides along edge of saw table.

Miter gauge with extension

Saw table

CUTTING DADOES

Miter gauge

With a single blade, make repeated cuts.

Single cut with dado blade

RADIAL ARM SAW

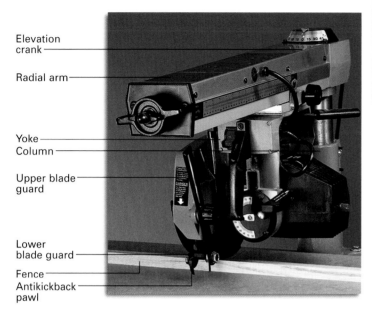

Elevation crank

Radial arm

Yoke

Column

Upper blade guard

Lower blade guard

Fence

Antikickback pawl

A RADIAL ARM SAW CAN...

■ Accurately crosscut and trim to length
■ Rip wood to width
■ Cut dadoes, rabbets, and grooves
■ Cut angles and bevels

A radial arm saw is much like a portable circular saw secured to an overhead trolley. The blade is attached to the motor arbor and is driven directly. The motor hangs over the work in a saddle called a *yoke*, which rotates 360 degrees. The motor also tilts 180 degrees within the yoke. The yoke itself slides from front to back on an overhead arm, which itself can be swung and locked into any position in its arc.

A radial arm saw will make the same cuts as a table saw, though rip cutting is more difficult and dangerous. It is easier and safer to crosscut long boards on a radial arm saw than on a table saw, however. A radial arm saw can be outfitted with accessories for other tasks, such as drum sanding. A radial arm saw takes up about the same working space as a table saw, and all the moving parts require more setup, tuning, and adjustments to keep the saw cutting accurately. Properly maintained and carefully used, however, a radial arm saw will provide satisfactory results.

BUYING A RADIAL ARM SAW

A 12-inch blade is common for radial arm saws, although there are some 10-inch models available. A 10-inch saw usually has a 1½-hp motor and will make cuts 2¾ to 3 inches deep at 90 degrees, and 2¼ to 2½ inches deep at 45 degrees. Table depth and arm length affect the width of rip cuts and the width of material you can crosscut on the saw. Look for crosscut capability of at least 15½ inches.

Other features that will make working with the saw more comfortable include easy-to-

read scales, both left and right; smooth yoke movement across the arm; and an automatic blade brake. Prices for 10-inch saws start at a little less than $600, but the better saws will cost about $100 more. Prices for 12-inch models are dramatically higher, starting at roughly twice the price of a 10-inch saw. Several companies offer reconditioned saws. As with other tools, buy the best you can afford.

SETTING UP THE SAW

A radial arm saw requires more initial setup and adjustment than a table saw. The most common tune-up procedures are shown on page 59. Since functional details vary among different saw models, be sure to read the manufacturer's instructions before setting up or using this tool.

When you're ready to saw, keep the following standard practices in mind.
■ Always mark the cut line on the workpiece.

CARE AND CLEANING

Although a radial arm saw has few motions, it is a fairly complicated piece of machinery. All parts have to work together smoothly and that means they have to be free of dirt and rust. After each use, blow out sawdust from the recesses with compressed air (wearing eye protection). Then clean the major assemblies of the saw.

Clean the column by raising it as high as it will go. Remove any rust with a plastic abrasive pad (not steel wool—it leaves steel threads behind), apply a thin coat of light machine oil or water-dispersing lubricant, raise and lower the arm a couple of times, and wipe the excess lubricant off so it won't attract dirt and sawdust.

Do the same for the roller track and bearings, using a 50-50 water-ammonia solution and cotton rags (paper towels will leave some residue behind).

To minimize your cleaning chores, hook your radial arm saw up to a good dust-collection system.

To change blades, clamp a 2×4 to the table and lower the arm until the blade bites solidly into it. Raise or remove the upper blade guard and remove the arbor nut. Install a new blade and tighten the nut.

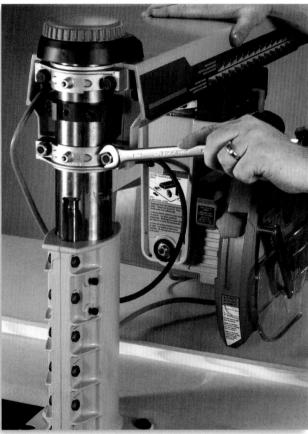

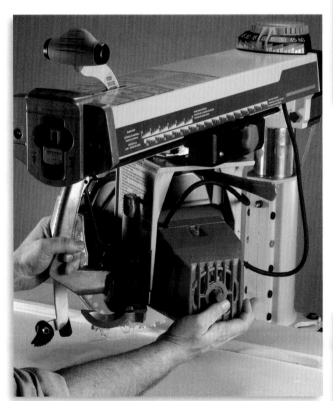

Tighten the clamp that holds the arm to the column when you can move the arm up and down on the column. On some models the clamp is secured with a hex-head bolt. On others you tighten an allen-head bolt.

If the column moves in the base when you push up on the arm, tighten the split casing bolt, but not so tight as to restrict the vertical movement of the column. If the column rotates in the base, tighten the column bar bolt.

Clamp the arm between 45 and 90 degrees, then push on the arm. If the arm moves freely, it's too loose. If it doesn't move at all, it's too tight. Tighten or loosen the clamp until the arm moves with moderate pressure.

Tighten the yoke clamp between rip and crosscut positions and try to rotate the motor. It should not move. Tighten the clamp to secure the motor. Tilt the motor between 45-and 90-degree bevels, and tighten the clamp. If the motor moves, tighten the clamp some more.

Place a square on the table and against the blade—between the teeth. If the square is not flush against the blade, adjust the motor. On most saws this requires loosening the motor mounting bolts.

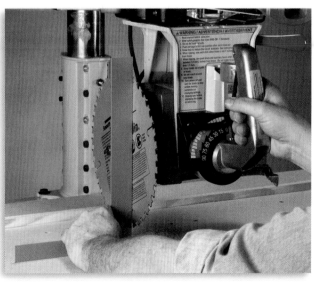

RADIAL ARM SAW

continued

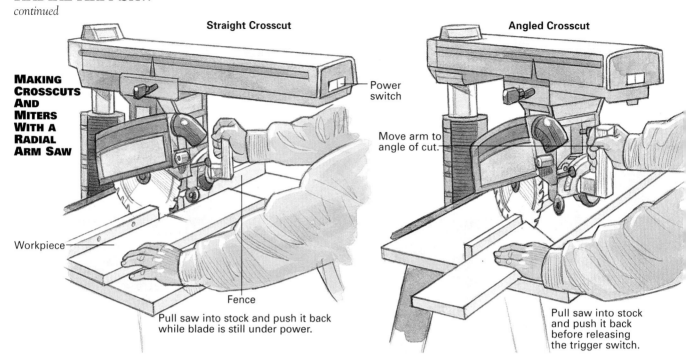

MAKING CROSSCUTS AND MITERS WITH A RADIAL ARM SAW

Straight Crosscut

Power switch

Workpiece

Fence

Pull saw into stock and push it back while blade is still under power.

Angled Crosscut

Move arm to angle of cut.

Pull saw into stock and push it back before releasing the trigger switch.

■ Always support long stock adequately on both the infeed and outfeed sides.
■ Cut with the finished side up to minimize tearout on the good side.
■ Set the blade so it cuts about ⅛ inch into the wooden table surface.
■ Make preliminary cuts at the angles and bevels you'll use before cutting the workpiece.
■ Replace the wooden fence often.

CROSSCUTS, MITERS, AND BEVELS

Crosscutting is the job this saw performs best. Miter cuts and bevel cuts are also easy to do with the radial arm saw.

RADIAL ARM SAW SAFETY

Because its blade is more exposed than blades on other saws, a radial arm saw demands special respect when it comes to safety.
■ Always wear safety glasses/goggles or a full face shield.
■ Stand to the handle side when crosscutting, with one hand on the saw and the other keeping the work snug against the fence. Never make freehand cuts and always return the blade completely to the rear of the saw table before removing any stock.
■ When ripping, feed the work against the direction of saw-blade rotation. Never rip cut without the splitter and antikickback devices in place.
■ Make sure the head is locked securely before making any kind of cut.
■ Unplug the saw when servicing or adjusting.

■ **MAKING CROSSCUTS:** Mark the cutting line on the workpiece, then place it snugly against the fence in line with the blade. Slide the blade forward to the line for a positioning check, then slide it back and turn the power on. With one hand holding the workpiece against the fence and the other on the saw handle, pull the saw completely forward, then push it back behind the fence. Since the blade rotates clockwise, it will tend to pull itself into the work and toward you, so keep your arm slightly stiff.
■ **MITER CUTS:** The workpiece remains stationary, so the potential for error is less with a radial arm saw than with a table saw. For smoother cuts, make the cut in two passes, the first one about 1/16 inch too long.

After marking the cut line, loosen the arm and rotate it to the desired angle. Lock the arm in place and set the work against the fence. Start the saw and cut as you would a crosscut. If the work is flat, and you need the same angle on the other end, flip the stock and repeat the cut. For moldings, move the arm to the same angle on the other side of the table.
■ **BEVEL CUTS:** Bevels are crosscuts made with the blade tilted. Lock the motor assembly at the bevel angle and clamp the work against the fence. Pull and return the blade slowly—the saw is cutting more wood and is working harder.

To make a compound miter, combine the techniques for miters and bevels. Set the arm

first and then the bevel angle.
Test the cut in scrap first.

MAKING RIP CUTS

Rip cutting is not a strength of a
radial arm saw. The cut is difficult
to control and dangerous—the saw
wants to throw the work back at
you. Radial arm saws come with
antikickback pawls or fingers, which
are made to prevent the stock from
flying back. If you have another tool
that will rip cut—a table saw, for
example—use it instead.

To make a rip cut, set and lock
the motor at 90 degrees to the arm.
Lock the yoke onto the arm at the
width of the cut.
Drop the
antikickback pawl
so it will engage the
stock at the proper
depth. Keep the
work flat on the
table and snug
against the fence,
and always use a
push stick to push
the work behind
the blade.

RIP CUTTING WITH A RADIAL ARM SAW

Motor locked at 90°

Anti-kickback pawl digs into surface of stock and helps keep saw action from kicking work back

Straightedge rides on edge of saw table.

Fence

Direction of feed

Workpiece

To make rip cuts, lock the motor at 90°, turn the motor on, and feed the work into the saw.

CUTTING BEVELS AND ANGLES

Cutting a Bevel

Blade angle scale adjusted to angle of bevel

Cutting an Angle

Arm rotated to angle of cut

For a compound miter, adjust blade-angle scale to bevel angle and rotate arm to miter angle.

CUTTING RABBETS AND DADOES

A dado blade will cut rabbets and dadoes to the correct width in one pass, but you can cut them with a standard blade. Make several passes until you reach the correct width and depth. Cut the outside edges first, then the middle.

Dado

Rabbet

Depth line

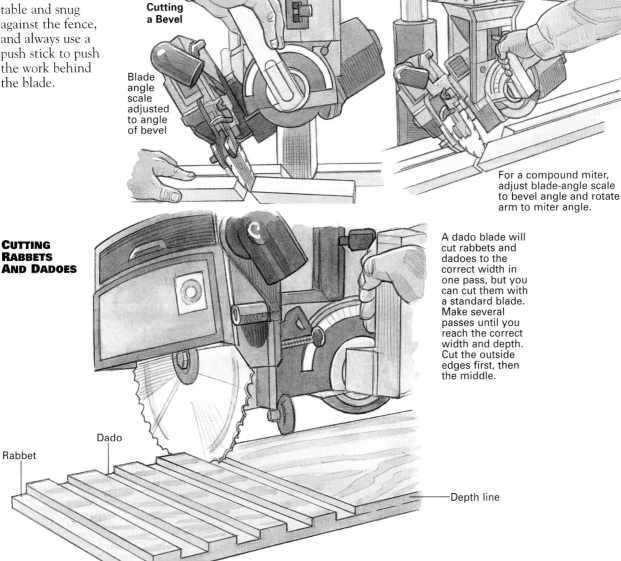

MITER SAW

Miter saws come in three different styles. A standard miter saw, far left, makes crosscuts and miter cuts. The tilting blade on a compound miter saw, left, adds bevel-cutting capacity. A sliding compound miter saw, below left, can cut wider stock than the other saws.

There's probably nothing more disappointing to a do-it-yourselfer than patiently miter-cutting moldings only to find the corners don't fit. Power miter saws (sometimes called *chop saws*) can alleviate some of those disappointments. They'll zip through picture-frame moldings, door and window trim, crown moldings, framing lumber—virtually anything that requires crosscuts, miter cuts, or bevel cuts. They make smooth, accurate cuts for joints that look like they were done by a pro.

Power miter saws are a cousin to the radial arm saw, but they're easier to set up, more accurate, and safer. They do have some limitations, however. Standard miter saws, the first generation of these versatile machines, won't cut compound miters or dadoes. The second-generation tool, the compound miter saw, will cut compound miters, but not dadoes. A sliding compound miter saw will do it all. None of them, however, will rip-cut like a radial arm saw, but that's a task you can do better with a table saw or circular saw. Some manufacturers make cordless miter saws.

MITER-SAW CHARACTERISTICS

The three kinds of miter saws have common design elements as well as differences.

■ **MOTOR MOUNTING:** In all three styles, the motor-and-blade unit mounts above the work on a pivot that allows the blade to be lowered into the cut. Many conventional miter saws allow perpendicular movement only. The motor tilts on a compound miter saw; it cuts bevels and miters. The tilting motor-blade unit of a sliding compound miter saw slides forward and back, greatly increasing its cutting capacity.

■ **FENCES AND TABLES:** Fences on all three models are permanently mounted to the base. They don't move or slide. Instead, the angle of the cut is controlled by the position of the table and the motor, which rotate and lock into position together. Rotating the table and motor sets the blade at the angle to the workpiece against the fence.

All miter saw tables rotate to at least 45 degrees to the left and right; some models exceed that limit by as much as 6 to 15 degrees, a handy feature for trim work—rooms are seldom perfectly square.

Fences are split on these saws to allow the blade to pass through. One or both of the fence sides are angle-cut in the opening if the saw will cut bevels. Taller fences support wider work.

A MITER SAW CAN...

■ Square board ends
■ Cut specific angles, miters, and compound miters with precision
■ Crosscut small and medium-size stock

■ **ANGLE SCALES:** These saws have positive detents at 0, 45, and 90 degrees. For precise work, look for a saw that lets you set the miter and bevel angles at less than a full degree without slipping back into a detent. Make sure both scales have large, easy-to-read numerals and markings.

■ **HANDLES:** The D-handle is the most common handle style; it may be mounted vertically or horizontally, depending on the model. Both have the trigger switch mounted under your index finger. Some users say the horizontal D-handle is easier to use and gives better control.

■ **BLADE SIZE:** Blade sizes on conventional saws range from 8¼ to 15 inches in diameter. A 12-inch blade is the largest for a compound miter saw. Bigger blades in the nonsliding models mean you can cut wider, thicker stock. A sliding compound miter saw can cut wide stock, even with a smaller blade. An 8½-inch blade on a sliding compound miter saw can cut across a 12-inch board. Larger blade diameter demands a more powerful motor and a heftier price.

Some models feature a blade brake, which speeds up multiple cuts because you don't have to wait for the blade to stop spinning on its own—a feature that adds convenience and safety. Buy the saw with the largest capacity you can afford—generally a 12-inch sliding compound miter saw will fit most home-workshop needs.

■ **BLADE GUARD:** Guards on conventional machines are usually adequate. Guards on the compound and sliding compound machines are more substantial. Make sure the guards retract smoothly.

■ **MATERIALS AND CONSTRUCTION:** Part of a miter saw's appeal is portability; most of them weigh from about 40 to 60 pounds. Material and construction quality vary from machine to machine. Make sure the saw movements are smooth and that there's no play in the joints. Extensive use of aluminum keeps weight down. If your saw will be on a bench or in one place most of the time, a heavier one may be acceptable. Mounting the saw on a solid work surface will make it seem more rigid.

■ **SLIDE RAILS:** Rails for sliding compound miter saws vary from model to model. Saws may have one, two, or three tubes or rails for the sliding carriage that holds the motor and blade. The carriage rides on linear bearings, which should move smoothly, without play.

The rails make sliding compound saws harder to transport and require more room at the rear; a standard 24-inch-deep worktable may not be deep enough for some saws. If you need portability, make sure you can lock and unlock the carriage conveniently.

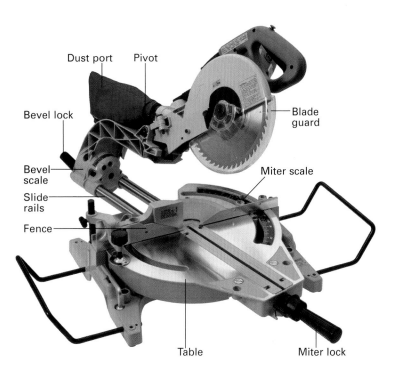

Dust port · Pivot · Blade guard · Bevel lock · Bevel scale · Slide rails · Fence · Miter scale · Table · Miter lock

■ **DUST PORT:** A miter saw should have a dust port, which you can easily hook up to your dust-collection system. These saws spit out lots of sawdust. Most come with a dust bag that can be installed when the saw isn't connected to a dust-collection system. The bag must be emptied frequently to maintain any effectiveness.

BLADES

Because miter saws are engineered for precision work, you have to be a little fussier in matching the blade to the saw and the work. Blades for miter saws are made differently from table saw or radial arm saw blades. Miter saws are for making precision crosscuts rather than ripping and rough crosscutting, so their teeth are machined with a straight or slightly reclining (*negative rake*) tooth face. Teeth on a table saw combination blade lean forward. Here are some tips on blade selection:

■ **8½-INCH BLADES** Use a 24- to 30-tooth blade for rough work, a 60-tooth one for finish cuts.

■ **10-INCH BLADES** Use a 40-tooth blade for rough work and a 60- to 80-tooth one for smooth cuts.

■ **12-INCH BLADES** Use a 60-tooth blade for rough cuts and an 80- to 96-tooth one for finish work.

Buy a carbide-tipped blade. A carbide-tipped blade, though more expensive than a steel one, can last almost 60 times as long as a steel blade. The net result is less cost per cut. Generally it's best to avoid thin-kerf blades—they tend to warp and wander. For dado work get a carbide-tipped blade with a raker tooth, which cleans out the bottom of the cut and keeps it from looking ragged.

MITER SAW
continued

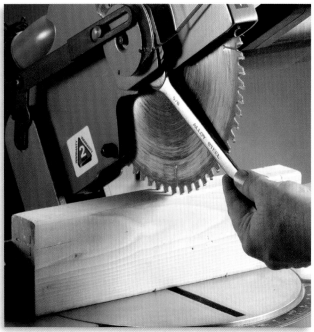

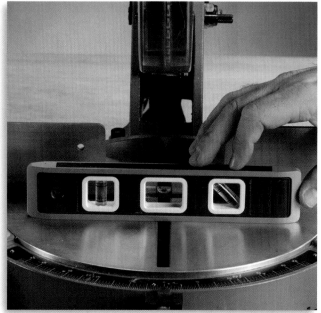

The miter saw's table and fence must be level and parallel to a plane through the blade's horizontal center line. Make sure the saw is on a level surface before making this adjustment.

Procedures for changing a miter saw blade vary from saw to saw, but generally involve immobilizing the blade, raising or removing the blade guard, and removing the arbor nut. Refer to your owner's handbook for specific instructions.

COSTS

Buying the right miter saw calls for careful analysis of your needs. A 10-inch conventional saw (starting at about $120) will handle most crosscut work for stock up to about a 2×6. At 45 degrees, it will cut through about 2×3 stock. Stepping up to a 12-inch conventional saw (a good one costs about $250) can increase your cutting capacities by as much as 40 percent. But for about the same price—or maybe $50 more—you can buy a high-quality 12-inch compound miter saw with an extra 2 to 2½ inches of cutting capacity.

Sliding compound miter saw prices start at about $350 and go up to more than $1,200. Several high-quality 10-inch models are available in the $500 to $600 range, and good 12-inch saws cost about $700.

USING YOUR POWER MITER SAW

Miter saws are designed for minimum setup and quick, efficient use. Although different cuts require different adjustments, the following tips apply to all cuts.

■ With one hand holding the work snugly on the fence, grasp the handle of the saw, squeeze the trigger, and lower the blade into the work. On a sliding compound miter saw, bring the blade out to the work and then lower it.

■ Let the saw come to full speed before bringing the blade into the work. Then let it come to a full stop before removing it from

the cut. Pulling a spinning blade back through the work can splinter the surfaces and throw the cutoff block at you.

■ Lower the blade and feed it into the work at a constant rate.

■ Mark the cut line on the work and whittle your way to it. Make the first cut about ¹⁄₁₆ inch away from the line, then trim the waste to the line with successive cuts. If necessary, make adjustments to the angle as you approach the final cut.

■ Support long stock with planks or stands. Molding or thin trim that extends more than a foot beyond the table ends will bow on the cutting surface. Supporting the ends keeps it flat on the table. Make sure the top of the blocks or stands is exactly the same height as the top of the table. If most of your work will be with long stock, build a permanent long table from ¾-inch plywood.

■ Clamp small workpieces to the fence to keep them from creeping off the mark.

■ The width of stock you can cut with a conventional or compound miter saw depends on how far down the blade pivots, among other design factors. (If the saw could cut to the middle of the blade, you could saw through material as wide as the diameter of the blade. No saw does this.) On some saws you can make a wider cut by raising the workpiece above the table so the blade is wider where it cuts into the wood. Place scrap wood on the saw table to make an auxiliary table to raise the workpiece. Use 1× scrap for 2× work, thicker scrap for thinner stock. You also can cut wider stock by double-cutting it—cutting one side, then the other. To do this successfully, position the blade precisely on the waste side of the cutting line on both ends.

■ Use a stop block to help you make several cuts to a consistent length—door stiles, spindles, or chair legs, for example.

You can add stop blocks (tack them down) to your support blocks, or adapt designs that fit your miter saw workstation. Both the stop block and its support must be securely anchored so they won't be jarred out of place when the workpiece slides up to it. For small work, use a homemade adjustable stop block similar to the one shown for use on a table-saw fence. (See the illustration page 56.)

MITER-SAW SAFETY

Miter saws, like all other power tools, require eye and ear protection. Keep your hands from beneath the blade—spinning or stopped. In addition, observe the following safety precautions:

■ Attach the saw to a waist-high work surface or to a ½-inch piece of plywood when carrying it to the work site. Clamp the plywood to a waist-high surface; don't operate the saw on the ground.

■ Always keep blades sharp and let the saw reach its operating speed before coming into contact with the work.

■ With one hand on the trigger switch and the other on the work, hold the workpiece firmly against the fence—pieces cut freehand can quickly become unguided missiles.

■ Avoid holding pieces that put your hand in danger—clamp small work to the fence before cutting.

■ After a cut, keep your hand on the handle until the blade comes to a full stop.

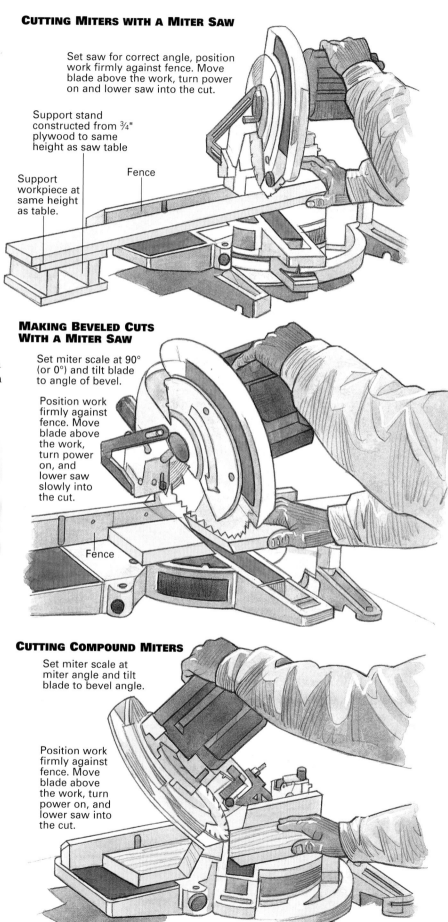

CUTTING MITERS WITH A MITER SAW

Set saw for correct angle, position work firmly against fence. Move blade above the work, turn power on and lower saw into the cut.

Support stand constructed from ¾" plywood to same height as saw table

Fence

Support workpiece at same height as table.

MAKING BEVELED CUTS WITH A MITER SAW

Set miter scale at 90° (or 0°) and tilt blade to angle of bevel.

Position work firmly against fence. Move blade above the work, turn power on, and lower saw slowly into the cut.

Fence

CUTTING COMPOUND MITERS

Set miter scale at miter angle and tilt blade to bevel angle.

Position work firmly against fence. Move blade above the work, turn power on, and lower saw into the cut.

BAND SAW

Cutting curves is easy with a band saw. By tilting the table, as shown above, you can cut curved, complex shapes like this toy boat hull.

CHOOSING THE RIGHT BAND-SAW BLADE

Width of Blade	Minimum Cutting Radius
$1/8$ inch	$1/8$ to $1/4$ inch
$3/16$ inch	$5/16$ to $1/2$ inch
$1/4$ inch	$3/8$ to $3/4$ inch
$3/8$ inch	1 to $1^{1}/16$ inches
$1/2$ inch	$1^{1}/4$ to $2^{1}/2$ inches

The minimum radius a blade will cut depends on its width and the set of the cutting teeth (the amount they are turned from the central axis of the blade). Blades with teeth set farther cut a wider kerf and will turn sharper corners—the radii at the lower end of the ranges shown above. To measure a radius quickly, use common objects—the radius of a pencil eraser is about $1/8$ inch; a dime, about $5/16$ inch; a penny, about $3/8$ inch; and a quarter, about $1/2$ inch.

A BAND SAW CAN...

- Cut curves and circles quickly
- Make angled and bevel cuts
- Resaw thick stock into thinner pieces
- Make templates

A band saw cuts with a blade that's been welded into a continuous loop. It makes both straight and curved cuts. With the exception of plunge cuts, a band saw does about the same jobs as a handheld jigsaw. The band saw is usually faster and is better for delicate work. A band saw is ideal for cutting intricate shapes, and it's the best tool for resawing—cutting a thick board lengthwise into thinner stock. Special wide blades are made for resawing.

The continuous band-saw blade loops around two wheels. (Some saws have three wheels, shown in the photograph at the bottom of the opposite page.) The teeth of the blade point down, which helps hold the work to the table. Above and below the table, guides keep the blade from wandering and twisting. The table tilts on most band saws for compound cutting.

BAND-SAW SIZES

Band saws are manufactured as both benchtop and stationary models. Size is indicated by either the widest piece the saw will cut or the thickest. Many manufacturers use wheel diameter as a measure of size; others list the throat depth of the saw—the distance from the blade to the rear housing. And some designate size as the maximum height the blade guide can be raised above the table. Make sure you know which criteria are being used when comparing one saw to another. Wheel diameter, especially, can be misleading—the throat depth is often slightly

BLADE GUIDES

Two sets of guides, above and below the table, keep the band-saw blade on course. Each has three elements—a thrust bearing, attached to the guide post, rides against the rear of the blade and keeps it in position only when you feed work into the cut, and two roller bearings keep the blade on track from side to side.

Most standard-equipment blade guides wear out quickly and will need to be replaced. Aftermarket guides come in different qualities. Graphite-impregnated guides are the minimum step-up you should consider, although you will be adjusting and replacing them more often than ball-bearing guides. Ball-bearing guides are more expensive—about 10 times more costly than graphite-impregnated models—but will repay you in longer-lasting blades, less-frequent adjustment, and more-accurate cuts.

Wheel guard
Tension control
Guide post
Guide post lock
Blade guard
Throat depth
Upper blade guides
Switch
Table
Lower blade guide
Dust port

less than the actual diameter of the wheel.

Three-wheel band saws (most common in benchtop models) offer greater throat depth than a similar-size two-wheel saw. Adjusting blade tracking to keep the blade from coming off the wheels is sometimes more difficult on a three-wheel saw. The frames on some three-wheel models are less rigid, and the increased flexing of the blade around three smaller-radius corners may make blades wear out or break more quickly.

Home-shop band saws usually have motors in the ½- to 1½-hp range. A ½-hp saw is standard and adequate for most work, except resawing thick stock. If resawing wood is one of the primary purposes for your purchase, you should look at saws with ¾- or 1-hp motors. If the tool specifications list peak horsepower, figure the working power at about 75 percent of that.

the left due to the position of the lower wheel. A tilting table is a good feature, allowing easy setup of angle cuts. Band saw tables are usually small. The table should have a slot for a miter gauge.

A benchtop saw is more portable than a stationary machine, which is handy if you have to tuck it into a corner in a small shop. Benchtop models in the 8- to 9-inch range usually have fractional-horsepower motors— ⅕ to ⅓ hp. Resaw capacity for benchtop saws ranges from 3¾ to about 5 inches.

No matter what style saw you buy, look for sturdy construction and a rigid frame— movement or flexing of any part of a band saw under a load will affect blade tension and accuracy. Machined steel or aluminum wheels are considered better than synthetic ones, and easy-to-adjust tensioning, tracking, blade guides, and bearings are essential.

Most band saws have two wheels. A compact three-wheel band saw (bottom photo) boasts a throat depth equal to a larger two-wheel saw. The blade path takes tight turns around the small wheels, limiting the width of the blade the saws can use. The less-rigid frame makes tensioning a wider blade difficult too.

STATIONARY VS. BENCHTOP

Stationary band saws are large machines, with sizes starting at 12 inches, going up to 36-inch professional-use saws. For general home-workshop use, a 14-inch saw will meet your needs. A 14-inch saw will cut stock up to 6 inches thick (even some 10-inch saws have a resawing capacity of 7 inches). If you'll be cutting pieces thicker than that, you can purchase a riser kit for many models. A riser kit is a cast block that bolts between the saw base and frame to increase its height. Larger blade guards come with it, and of course, you'll need a longer blade. A riser kit can increase your cutting depth to 12 inches, but make sure your band saw's motor is up to the heavy sawing.

Most, but not all, band saw tables are built to tilt to the right and left, with less tilt on

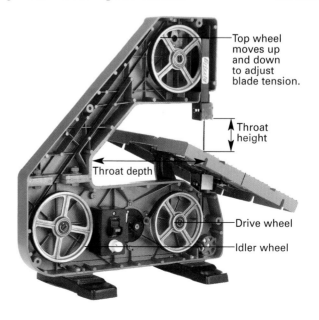

Top wheel moves up and down to adjust blade tension.
Throat height
Throat depth
Drive wheel
Idler wheel

BAND SAW
continued

To install a new blade, remove the blade guards and throat plate, and loosen the thrust and roller bearings. Release the tension on the upper wheel and pull the blade toward you. With the teeth of the new blade facing you, install it over the wheels. Adjust the tension while rotating wheels.

Adjust tension for blade width

Blade teeth point down

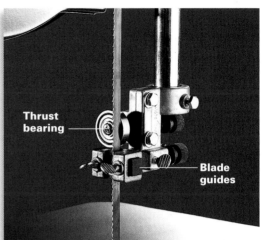

Thrust bearing

Blade guides

Band-saw guides do not contact the blade when it is running free, only when the work pushes the blade into them. Insert a fresh dollar bill or piece of 20-lb. paper between the blade and the guides when adjusting them. Make sure that the upper and lower guides allow the blade to track vertically and the roller guides do not contact the teeth.

COSTS

Good brand-name benchtop band saws are available for about $180. Shopping for a few more features and increased rigidity will bring the price up to around $260, and for another $100 you can get a 10-inch benchtop model with full features and a ½-hp motor. A large benchtop model isn't for you if you're looking for portability, though. At almost 70 pounds, the larger saw's weight is about twice that of the average benchtop model.

A stationary 10- or 12-inch band saw with an open-leg stand costs around $300. Prices for 14-inch saws run from about $350 to well over $700, but you can probably find a band saw that meets most home-shop needs for somewhere between $350 and $500.

BAND-SAW BLADES

Choosing the band-saw blade for your job is relatively easy. The radius of the cut you want to make determines the maximum width of the blade you can use. (See "Choosing the Right Band-Saw Blade," page 66.) Whether you are crosscutting or rip cutting will influence the type of blade tooth. Either a regular- or skip-tooth blade works well across the grain. Raker-tooth blades are better for cutting with the grain. Hook-tooth blades are aggressive blades that work well for resawing. In general, choose a narrow blade with more teeth per inch (tpi) for curved cuts and a wide blade with fewer tpi for straight cuts and resawing. The blade should always have at least three teeth in the thickness of the stock. A ¼-inch blade with 10 to 14 tpi is a good choice for general sawing.

Guide post

Upper blade guides

The upper guides of a band saw are held in the guide post, which can be raised or lowered to accept different thicknesses of wood. Before sawing, adjust the guide post so it's about ⅜" above the surface of the workpiece.

To increase blade life and make cutting curves easier, round the back of your blade with a coarse stone. The round surface wears less on thrust bearings and rides smoothly in the saw kerf. Run the saw for about a minute with the stone on one edge, then the other. Then round off the back.

MAKING CROSSCUTS WITH A BAND SAW

STRAIGHT CROSSCUT

Miter gauge with extension

ANGLED CUT

Miter gauge set for angle of cut

BEVELED CUT

Tilt table to make beveled cuts.

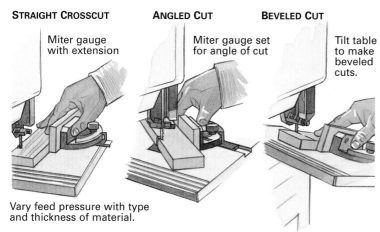

Vary feed pressure with type and thickness of material.

RESAWING

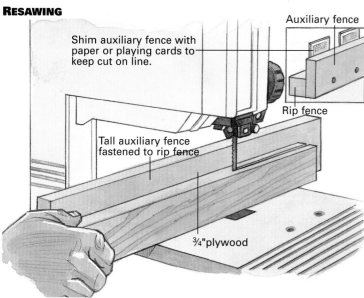

Shim auxiliary fence with paper or playing cards to keep cut on line.

Auxiliary fence

Rip fence

Tall auxiliary fence fastened to rip fence

¾" plywood

RIP CUTTING WITH A BAND SAW

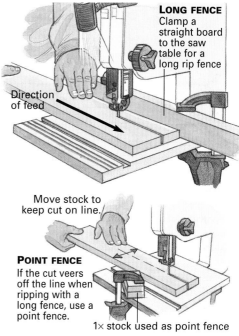

LONG FENCE
Clamp a straight board to the saw table for a long rip fence

Direction of feed

Move stock to keep cut on line.

POINT FENCE
If the cut veers off the line when ripping with a long fence, use a point fence.

1× stock used as point fence

CUTTING CIRCLES WITH A BAND SAW

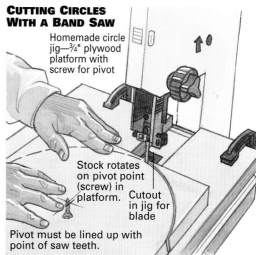

Homemade circle jig—¾" plywood platform with screw for pivot

Stock rotates on pivot point (screw) in platform. Cutout in jig for blade

Pivot must be lined up with point of saw teeth.

MAKING RELIEF CUTS

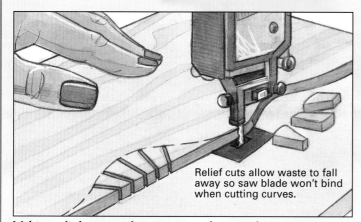

Relief cuts allow waste to fall away so saw blade won't bind when cutting curves.

Making relief cuts can keep you out of a jam when cutting curves and tight corners. After outlining the final contour of your cut, make several straight cuts from the edge to the contour line—the tighter the corner, the closer together the relief cuts. Then, cut the contour line. The waste at the relief cuts will fall away, leaving the blade to run freely around the turn.

BAND-SAW SAFETY

Band-saw blades travel at speeds of up to almost a mile a minute, and even though they are thin, they can be dangerous. Always wear eye protection and suitable ear protection. Though band saws run more quietly than other tools, constant exposure to noise can be harmful.

■ Keep blade guards closed when operating the saw and the blade guide adjusted to about ⅜ inch above the work being cut.

■ Keep blades sharp and properly tensioned. Loose or too-tight blades will break.

■ Hold the workpiece firmly against the fence, table, or miter gauge and use a slow, steady feed rate.

■ Use a push stick close to the blade.

SCROLL SAW

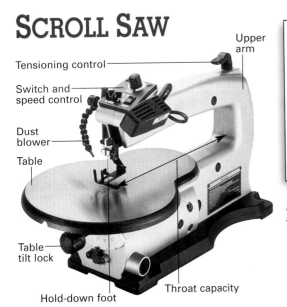

- Tensioning control
- Switch and speed control
- Dust blower
- Table
- Table tilt lock
- Hold-down foot
- Upper arm
- Throat capacity

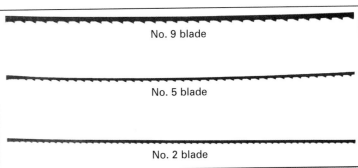

No. 9 blade

No. 5 blade

No. 2 blade

These three scroll-saw blades will handle most cutting. From top: No. 9 blade for thick material; No. 5 blade for material less than ¾ inch thick; No. 2 for intricate work in thin material.

A scroll saw is a coping saw with a motor on it. The saw's very thin blade travels up and down up to 2,000 strokes per minute between the motor and the head through a hole in the table. No other tool can cut curves, inlays, and fretwork as finely as the scroll saw.

Manufacturers classify scroll saws as both benchtop and floor models, a distinction that usually indicates whether the saw comes with legs or whether a stand costs extra. A saw without legs or a stand can be placed on a workbench. Weight varies widely; you'll find 98-pound saws in the benchtop category and 30-pound stationary models. Focus on the saw's features and the quality of its cuts when you are shopping.

Scroll-saw size (from 14 to 24 inches) indicates the deepest cut the saw will make—the distance from the back of the arm to the blade. Since a scroll saw is likely to be a tool you purchase with complicated projects in mind, buy the biggest you can afford. If you're in the market for a starter saw, get a 16-inch model. And no matter what size saw you're shopping for, look for these useful features.

■ **VARIABLE SPEED:** A speed control helps when cutting different kinds of materials.

■ **EASY BLADE CHANGING:** You'll change scroll-saw blades often; get the easiest blade-change mechanism you can find.

■ **PARALLEL ARMS:** The blade moves with a vertical rocking motion on this kind of saw. Vibration should be minimal on a well-engineered saw.

■ **DUST BLOWER:** Most saws have this; it keeps sawdust from obscuring your cut line.

■ **HOLD-DOWN FOOT DESIGN:** This is the claw, paw, or spring that holds the work down during cutting. It should be firm and stiff enough to hold the work, but relaxed enough that you can maneuver the work with slight pressure.

■ **TILT TABLE:** A tilting table is handy for some projects, such as inlays. Make sure the table stays in place when locked.

COSTS

Prices start at about $80 for a basic 16-inch scroll saw and increase to almost $1,000 for a top-of-the-line 24-inch model.

A SCROLL SAW CAN...

■ Make puzzles and jewelry
■ Saw intricate decorative fretwork

USING A SCROLL SAW

Scroll sawing requires skill and patience. A scroll saw cuts precisely, not quickly. Guide and feed the work steadily with both hands. Don't rush, but don't feed it too gingerly either. Feed speed is right when the blade produces a steady stream of sawdust. Move to the side of the table when a front position won't let you work smoothly, and turn the work so it's always moving against the front of the blade toward the rear of the table.

SCROLL-SAW BLADES

Selecting the right blade is a key element in scroll sawing.

The first difference you'll note in scroll-saw blades is how they mount. Pin-end blades have a perpendicular pin that hooks into the blade holder. Plain-end blades are flat and need to be tightened into the holder. Pin-end blades are the quick-change artist of the two, but the pin might not fit through the small blade start hole required for very delicate cuts. Plain-end blades take more time to change but are more versatile. Many saws will accept any style with adapters.

Choosing the right blade means balancing several factors, the type and thickness of the material and the delicacy of the curves you're cutting, for example. Scroll blades come with several variations.
■ Skip-tooth blades have teeth missing to allow quicker ejection of sawdust.
■ Reverse-tooth blades have teeth that cut upward; they make smoother cuts.
■ Spiral blades have teeth twisted around the central axis. They're good for tight turns, but they leave a wider kerf.

In general, use wide, coarse blades and slow speeds for heavy cutting; narrow, fine blades and faster speeds for thin stock and smooth cuts.

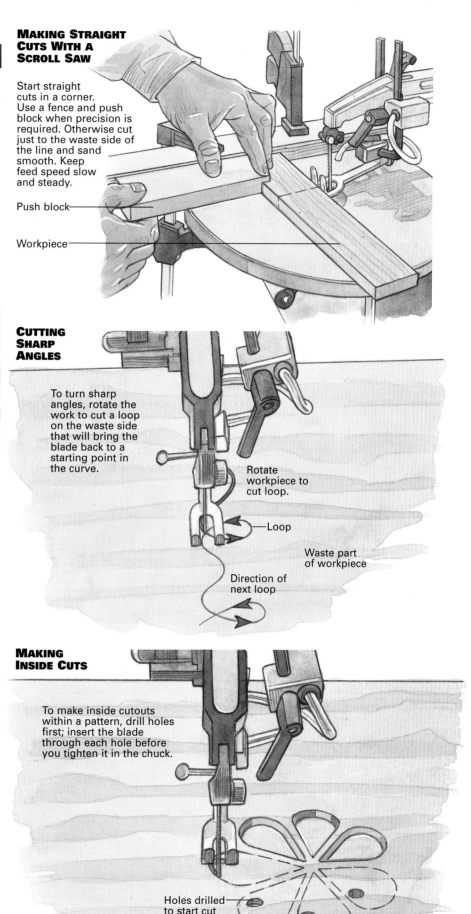

MAKING STRAIGHT CUTS WITH A SCROLL SAW

Start straight cuts in a corner. Use a fence and push block when precision is required. Otherwise cut just to the waste side of the line and sand smooth. Keep feed speed slow and steady.

Push block

Workpiece

CUTTING SHARP ANGLES

To turn sharp angles, rotate the work to cut a loop on the waste side that will bring the blade back to a starting point in the curve.

Rotate workpiece to cut loop.

Loop

Waste part of workpiece

Direction of next loop

MAKING INSIDE CUTS

To make inside cutouts within a pattern, drill holes first; insert the blade through each hole before you tighten it in the chuck.

Holes drilled to start cut

DRILL PRESS

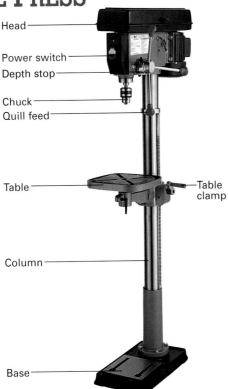

Head
Power switch
Depth stop
Chuck
Quill feed
Table
Table clamp
Column
Base

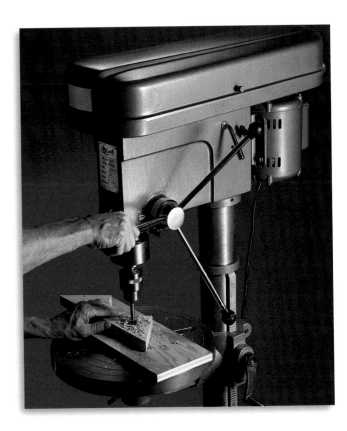

You can drill holes in many kinds of materials with a portable drill. But when it comes to drilling evenly spaced holes for cabinetry and shelves, drilling metal, drilling holes at precise angles, or boring large holes with a circle cutter, you need a drill press. With the right accessories, a drill press will double as a drum sander, planer, router, and mortiser.

A drill press is built for accuracy and power. Most models are driven by an induction motor and have a belt and stepped-pulley drive system that turns the spindle and chuck at speeds from about 150 to 4,700 rpm. You lower the bit into the work with a quill control, and the table moves up and down the column to accommodate workpieces of different thicknesses.

A DRILL PRESS CAN...

■ Accurately drill and bore small and large holes
■ Make repetitive, evenly spaced holes
■ Drill consistently to a specific depth
■ With accessories, sand curved surfaces
■ Drill angled holes
■ Cut mortises, dovetails, and box joints

DRILL PRESS FEATURES

Drill presses are made in three styles—benchtop, stationary, and radial. They all have the same basic features—scaled, of course, to their various sizes.

■ **QUILL TRAVEL** is a measure of how far the bit will travel from its stationary position to full depth.

Longer quill travels mean you can drill deeper holes. Quill travel starts at about 2 inches in benchtop models and reaches 6 inches in high-end presses. Midrange quill travel, 4 inches, will do most of the jobs you have in mind.

■ **DEPTH STOPS** limit quill travel to a preset depth. Make sure they operate quickly and accurately. Many owners find the threaded rod and stop mechanisms easier to use than those with rotating collars.

■ **VARIABLE SPEEDS** You'll need to change speeds as you change bits and materials. Speed changes are accomplished on most models by moving one or both ends of the belt(s) to different positions on stepped cone pulleys. You can change speeds electronically on some models—for a price. Look for 250 rpm or lower at the bottom of the speed scale if you'll be drilling hardwoods with Forstner bits, circle cutters, or large holesaws. For versatility with a full range of materials, get a speed of 3,000 rpm or higher at the top end (see "Drill Press Speeds," page 74). Check out the speed increments also—you'll want at least 12.

■ **POWER STARTS** out small in benchtop models, at about ⅙ hp, and tops out at about ¾ hp. Floor models are heftier, up to 1½ hp, but you won't need much more than ¾ hp in any drill press. A totally enclosed fan-cooled

(TEFC) motor is a good option; it is less affected by dust than an open motor.

■ **CAPACITY** is a measure of how wide a workpiece the drill press will accommodate. The standard measure of capacity is the distance between the bit and the column. Benchtop drill-press capacities start at 8 inches and run to 15 inches; stationary throat depths go from 13 to 22 inches. If you're like the majority of home-workshop operators, you will find a 15- to 17-inch capacity adequate. For large-capacity drilling, a radial drill press is useful. On these models, the head slides forward on an arm to accept large work. The head also tilts for drilling on an angle, but some radial drill presses suffer deflection from side pressure and won't keep the bit on track.

■ **CHUCK** sizes are ½, ⅝, and ¾ inch. A ½-inch chuck will handle almost everything in your woodworking shop, but sometimes large holes in metals call for a ⅝-inch chuck. A keyless chuck will cost more and you may not be able to close it tightly enough to keep the bit from slipping.

■ **TABLES** generally have open slots or closed T-slots; the latter are usually found on larger tables and often have a moat at the edge to collect cutting fluid—a useful feature if you anticipate much metal cutting. Open slots are desirable if you plan to attach an auxiliary wood table.

Tables should be cast iron and are made to ride up and down on the column; rack-and-pinion adjustments are far superior to sliding tables. A tilting table is handy for drilling angled holes, though it may not hold a precise setting through repeated drilling. Always double-check the angle before drilling.

■ **THE FINISH** on a drill press may tell you things about its overall quality that you can't measure, but you can make some judgments about frame rigidity and vibration. If possible, run the machine before you buy it; vibration should be imperceptible enough to not cause water to ripple in a cup. Link belts will often reduce vibration considerably more than standard V-belts.

Head slides forward and back and tilts.

Tilt clamp

RADIAL-ARM DRILL PRESS

To check the chuck runout, clamp a scrap block to the table and insert a know bit (available at your tool distributor) in the chuck. Rotate the chuck by turning the belt, and move the scrap until it just touches the bit. Rotate the chuck again until the bit pulls away from the wood. Measure the gap with a feeler gauge. If runout is not within manufacturer's specifications (.005 inch is very good), remove the chuck and measure spindle runout.

DRILL PRESS
continued

DRILL PRESS COSTS

You can buy a benchtop drill press for $80 or less. For that, you get a 4-inch throat (drill at the center of an 8-inch disc) and 2 inches of quill travel. Drill presses with a 10-inch capacity run from about $160 to $250, and 14-inch ones listed as benchtop models run to more than $1,000. At this stage you've added a lot of weight—to more than 100 pounds, which might seem contrary to what you want in a benchtop tool. For $220 to $280 you can buy a good-quality benchtop drill press.

Stationary models start at about $180 and go up to $1,000, but there are several models in the $300 to $400 range that will give you large capacities, more than 3 inches of quill travel, sufficient range of speeds, and plenty of power.

Radial drill presses retail for as little as $189, and at least two benchtop models are available in the $300 to $400 range. Expect to pay around $500 for the best floor models.

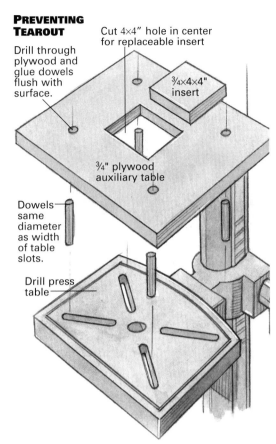

PREVENTING TEAROUT

Cut 4×4" hole in center for replaceable insert

¾×4×4" insert

Drill through plywood and glue dowels flush with surface.

¾" plywood auxiliary table

Dowels same diameter as width of table slots.

Drill press table

MORTISE MACHINE

Mortising machines are dedicated to one task—drilling square holes for mortise-and-tenon joints. They do what a mortising attachment on a drill press does, without the setup and take-down required by a drill press. Most models have easy-to-change bits to make mortises up to ½ inch wide and have induction motors of about ½ hp. These one-use drill presses start at about $200.

DRILL PRESS SPEEDS (RPM)

Drill Type	Softwood	Hardwood	Acrylic	Brass	Aluminum	Steel
Twist drills						
¹⁄₁₆"-³⁄₁₆"	3000	3000	2500	3000	3000	3000
¼"-³⁄₈"	3000	1500	2000	1200	2500	1000
⁷⁄₁₆"-⁵⁄₈"	1500	750	1500	750	1500	600
¹¹⁄₁₆"-1"	750	500	NR	400	1000	350
Brad-point drills						
⅛"	1800	1200	1500	NR	NR	NR
¼"	1800	1000	1500	NR	NR	NR
⅜"	1800	750	1500	NR	NR	NR
½"	1800	750	1000	NR	NR	NR
Spade bits						
¼"-½"	2000	1500	NR	NR	NR	NR
⅝"-1"	1750	1500	NR	NR	NR	NR
1⅛"-1½"	1500	1000	NR	NR	NR	NR
Spade bits with spurs						
⅜"-1"	2000	1800	500	NR	NR	NR
Holesaws						
1"-1½"	500	350	NR	250	250	NR
1⅝"-2"	500	250	NR	150	250	NR
2⅛"-2½"	250-500	NR	NR	150	250	NR

Speeds based on new bits drilling in face grain. In end grain, use slower speeds.
NR=Not Recommended

DRILLING TO A SPECIFIC DEPTH

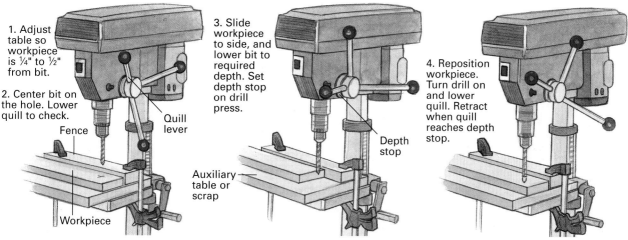

1. Adjust table so workpiece is ¼" to ½" from bit.

2. Center bit on the hole. Lower quill to check.

Fence

Quill lever

Workpiece

3. Slide workpiece to side, and lower bit to required depth. Set depth stop on drill press.

Auxiliary table or scrap

Depth stop

4. Reposition workpiece. Turn drill on and lower quill. Retract when quill reaches depth stop.

DRILLING ANGLED HOLES

Tilt table to angle of hole. Clamp a waste block to workpiece. Bit contacts waste block first, which steadies it in workpiece.

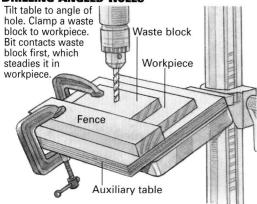

Waste block

Workpiece

Fence

Auxiliary table

DRILLING SPACED HOLES

1. Clamp a ruler to the fence, and place the workpiece against the fence. Drill the first hole. Turn off the drill press, keeping the bit in the workpiece. Then align the end of workpiece at an inch mark on the ruler.

Thin scrap same thickness as ruler, if ruler extends down fence behind work.

Ruler clamped to fence

Fence

Lay out individual hole locations on the workpiece, measuring from the end or the center, as appropriate.

2. Raise the bit and move the workpiece until the end aligns with the mark on the ruler indicating the required spacing (½", 1", etc.).

USING YOUR DRILL PRESS

Drill-press operation is not complicated, but accuracy requires careful setup.

■ Match the bit to the material you're drilling, and tighten it in the chuck. Set the appropriate speed. (See "Drill Press Speeds," opposite.)

■ Clamp a fence to the table so the work will be centered under the bit. Adjust the table until the bit is about ½ inch from the work surface. If you're drilling through the work, make sure the hole in the drill press table is centered on the bit.

■ Pull the quill toward the work and set the depth stop for partial holes. Retract the quill and re-center the workpiece, if necessary.

■ Turn the motor on and lower the bit slowly into the work.

■ Retract the bit when the depth stop reaches its limit. Let the bit stop before removing the workpiece.

■ When drilling steel ⅛ inch or thicker, lubricate the bit with oil.

DRILL-PRESS SAFETY

Don't be lulled into unsafe practices by the quiet movement of a drill press. In addition to keeping your fingers away from the bit and wearing eye protection, observe the following:

■ Always clamp the work. A bit can grab the workpiece and spin it violently.

■ Keep shirt sleeves, necklaces, and other adornments away from the bit and chuck. They may pull you into the machine before you can stop it.

■ Never use an auger with screw thread. They're made for slow drilling with a brace and bit, and the screw threads will pull themselves through the work.

MAKING A BLIND MORTISE

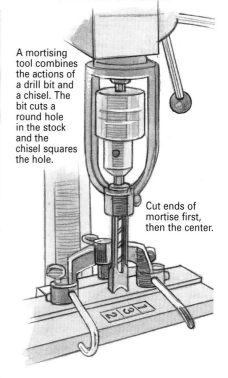

A mortising tool combines the actions of a drill bit and a chisel. The bit cuts a round hole in the stock and the chisel squares the hole.

Cut ends of mortise first, then the center.

JOINTER

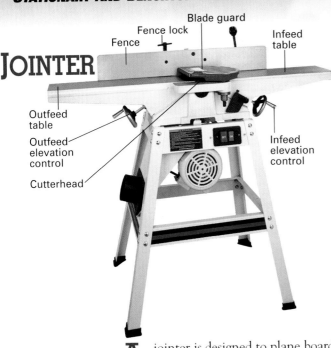

Fence lock

Blade guard

Fence

Infeed table

Outfeed table

Outfeed elevation control

Infeed elevation control

Cutterhead

A JOINTER CAN...

■ Plane edges so they are perfectly smooth and straight
■ Remove slight warps, twists, and cupping from boards
■ Taper, bevel, or chamfer stock
■ Cut rabbets

A jointer is designed to plane board edges smooth and straight. But you can press a jointer into other services—planing cabinet door edges; taking out saw marks; "uncupping" a warped board; making tapers, chamfers, and bevels; forming rabbets; and cleaning glue off joints.

Depending on the model, its cutterhead will contain two or three knives that rotate clockwise (when viewed from the front of the machine) at speeds from 5,000 to 7,000 rpm. The cutterhead is mounted between an infeed and outfeed table, with the infeed table (and on some models, the outfeed table, too) adjustable to different cutting depths. A fence keeps the workpiece straight, and a swiveling guard protects your fingers from the spinning blades.

BUYING A JOINTER

You'll find jointers in benchtop, cabinet-mounted, and open-stand models, in sizes from 4 to 16 inches. A 6-inch jointer (the knife length) is probably the minimum size for home-workshop versatility.

Benchtop jointers are good for tight spaces, but even with a 6-inch table they will not be as sturdy and accurate as their stationary cousins. Benchtop fences have a tendency to pivot, and you also might not care for the high-speed noise of their universal motors. Expect to pay from about $250 to $350 for a benchtop model with enough power and

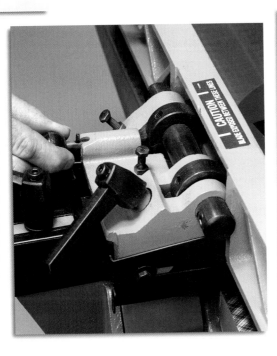

Your jointer owner's manual will show you how to adjust the fence position and square it to the table, both critical adjustments for true edges. For some operations, you'll have to tilt the fence in relation to the table.

JOINTER SAFETY

Jointer cutterheads can reach speeds of up to 7,000 rpm, and wood chips, and particles driven at that speed can cause serious injury. So can their sharp knives. Observe the following practices when using a jointer.
■ Always wear safety glasses or goggles and ear protection.
■ Keep your fingers away from the spinning blades—use jointer push blocks on any flat cut narrower than 5 inches. And don't attempt to use a jointer on stock less than 12 inches long. Joint longer pieces and cut the work to length.
■ Leave space at each end sufficient to allow feeding of long stock.
■ Unplug the motor when making adjustments.

stability to give you consistent joints.

Stationary jointers (from about $300 to $700 and more for a 6-inch model) will have induction motors in the range of $3/4$ to $1\frac{1}{2}$ hp. A $3/4$-hp motor on a 6-inch jointer will smooth oak and birch without complaining. Variable speeds can help match the cut to the personality of the wood.

Fences should be adjustable along the width of the table, to vary the width of the cut and equalize blade wear. You should also be able to adjust the angle of the fence. The taller the fence, the wider the piece you can stand on edge to plane. Fences with center locks will stay put better than those with other locking systems. And table locks with wheels are more precise than levers. Although the price range is wide, you can find a high-quality jointer priced from $550 to $600.

USING YOUR JOINTER

Jointers require initial and periodic adjustment. These procedures are shown in the operator's manual for the machine. The following represents techniques that are basic to all jointers.

■ Make cuts in several passes. Set your infeed table for a cut of $1/16$ inch in softwoods, shallower in hardwoods. Set the fence for the angle of the cut, recheck it, and tighten it.

■ Turn the power on and place the workpiece flat on the infeed table and flush with the fence. When possible, turn the grain so it faces down and toward you.

■ Grip the board with both hands and feed the work into the cutterhead at an even speed. Don't stop. When the work reaches the outfeed table, apply gentle pressure to keep the cut edge flat. To avoid chipping when planing against the grain, move the work slowly.

■ To flatten cupping in a board, set the cutting depth at $1/32$ inch and feed the work concave side down with a a push stick. Make several passes until the board is flat, then cut the crown off the other side with your table saw or band saw (see illustration, below right).

■ When cutting stock narrower than the full width of the cutterhead, vary the fence location to spread the wear evenly over the width of the knives.

PLANING AN EDGE

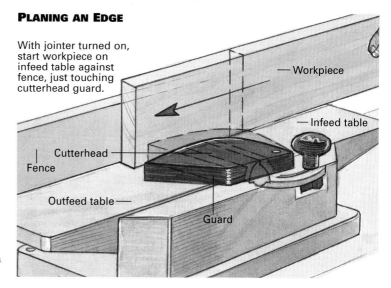

With jointer turned on, start workpiece on infeed table against fence, just touching cutterhead guard.

Workpiece — Infeed table — Cutterhead — Fence — Outfeed table — Guard

PLANING END GRAIN

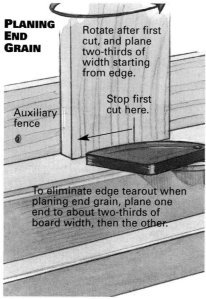

Rotate after first cut, and plane two-thirds of width starting from edge.

Stop first cut here.

Auxiliary fence

To eliminate edge tearout when planing end grain, plane one end to about two-thirds of board width, then the other.

PLANING A SURFACE

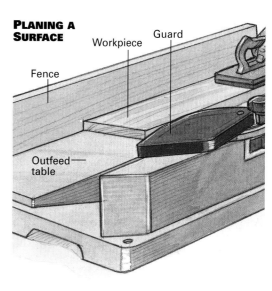

Workpiece — Guard — Fence — Outfeed table

FLATTENING A CUPPED BOARD

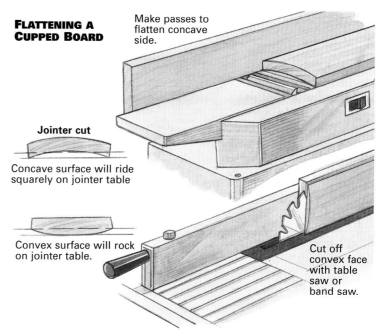

Make passes to flatten concave side.

Jointer cut

Concave surface will ride squarely on jointer table

Convex surface will rock on jointer table.

Cut off convex face with table saw or band saw.

BENCHTOP PLANER

A PLANER CAN...

- Plane boards to exact thicknesses
- Surface faces of rough stock

thing this tool relishes. You can use it to smooth out minor blemishes and saw marks, or to plane multiple boards that will be joined in a tabletop to uniform thickness.

Power planers—they're surfacing machines, really—have come a long way in 15 years. Once, even some shops run by pros didn't have room for a planer's large footprint or price tag. The benchtop model has changed all that, and recent innovations in their technology have all but removed their primary character flaw—the tendency to *snipe* the ends of boards. Snipe is a deeper cut within the last few inches at either end of the stock. Snipe drives woodworkers mad. Design and engineering advancements in many small planers have minimized sniping problems.

BUYING A PLANER

When shopping for a planer, take the following specifications and design characteristics into account:

■ **SIZE:** Planers are sized by the width of the cutterhead—the maximum width of stock they can accept. Cutterhead width of 12 or 12½ inches is common for portable benchtop planers. A 12½-inch planer should accomplish any planing you need to do in a home workshop. The maximum thickness a planer can handle is also worth noting. Most benchtop planers can handle 6-inch-thick boards. Some are limited to 5-inch stock.

With its cutterhead and universal motor screaming along at 8,000 to 10,000 rpm, a benchtop planer might sound more like a jet plane than a workshop tool. Shearing off up to ⅛-inch of a 12-inch-wide board is not quiet work.

Yet when your rough-sawn oak slides out of the planer ready for finish sanding, you won't mind the noise. Rough stock is not the only

■ **MINIMUM CUTTING DEPTH:** Planers are rated to cut from 3⁄32 to 3⁄16 inch deep, most at ⅛ inch. But this maximum cutting depth applies to stock that's 5 to 6 inches wide, not to stock of the maximum width the machine can accept. Usually you'll do very little planing with the cutterhead set to take the maximum cut. Better results come with multiple passes and shallower cuts.

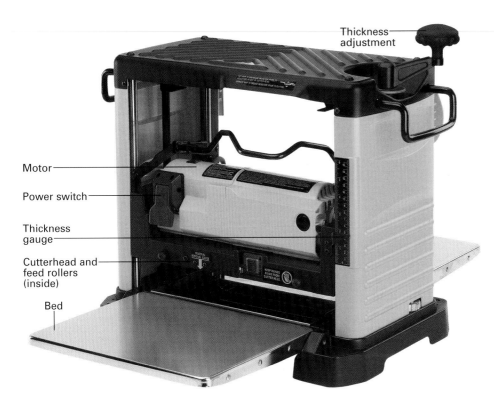

Thickness adjustment

Motor

Power switch

Thickness gauge

Cutterhead and feed rollers (inside)

Bed

Look for scales that are easy to read and controls that are easy to adjust and that stay put when set. Scales that show precise depth changes in 1/64-inch increments give you more control than coarser scales.

Only a couple of models feature a turret-style depth stop. Much like a plunge router depth stop, this feature comes in handy when planing several pieces to the same thickness.

■ **BED AND ROLLERS:** Benchtop planers are made mostly of stamped steel and cast aluminum to save weight. Most have polished steel tables of various gauges. Most benchtop planers weigh about 60 to 70 pounds, although a few weigh more. You may find a heavier tool acceptable if you don't have to move it frequently.

Some models come with table extensions equipped with infeed and outfeed rollers—a definite plus. A few have top rollers that allow you to slide a board easily across the top of the planer to feed through again. Rubber or rubber-coated feed rollers are common in benchtop models.

■ **CUTTERHEAD AND SUPPORT:** This is one aspect of benchtop planer construction that makes a big difference in performance. Cutterheads on most models have two knives, and no-load speeds average between 9,000 and 10,000 rpm. The speed can drop by 1,000 to 2,000 rpm when making a cut. Higher speeds usually mean smoother cuts.

The cutterhead moves up and down on four steel corner posts to set the cutting depth

on most benchtop planers. (One brand has a fixed cutterhead; the table moves to adjust cutting depth.) Four-post support or a fixed cutterhead keeps the cutterhead from rocking as the end of the workpiece passes under it, minimizing snipe. These designs are preferable to two-post cutterhead support found in older planers. Some of the four-post planers have a cutterhead lock too. On those machines, you adjust the head to the planing thickness desired, then flip a lever to clamp the cutterhead solidly to the posts. The lock further minimizes cutterhead movement to help reduce snipe.

A cutterhead lock, available on several models, combats snipe (a deeper cut at the board ends) by clamping the cutterhead to the uprights.

BIG PLANERS

Most planers larger than the benchtop models sell for $1,200 or more and weigh anywhere from 500 pounds to more than a ton. Even the middleweights that go for less than $1,000, like the one shown at right, tip the scales at 400 pounds or more.

They're formidable machines that can take a cut about twice the depth of a benchtop model in wider stock. They have three or more knives in the cutterhead and are powered by 2- to 5-hp motors. A few boast 7- to 10-hp motors. Most require a 220-volt electrical supply. All but a few have fixed cutterheads, adjustable cast-iron tables, serrated-steel infeed rollers, and polished-steel outfeed rollers. These big boys far exceed the needs of the weekend home hobbyist.

Even though they're not made for the casual user, however, a 15- or 20-inch model could be useful for a serious hobbyist who uses a lot of rough lumber or someone who runs a small commercial woodworking shop.

A 15-inch planer has larger capacity and more power than a benchtop planer, but isn't quite as hefty as the industrial-strength 20- and 24-inch machines.

BENCHTOP PLANER
continued

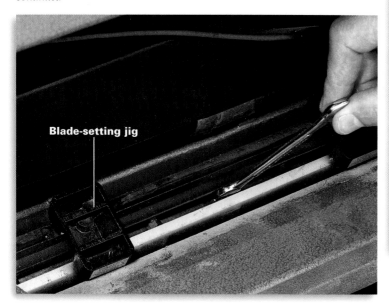

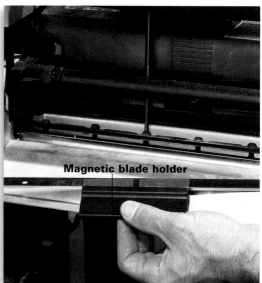

Procedures for adjusting knives will vary with each model. Many can be set using magnetic jigs like the ones shown here.

■ **KNIVES:** Here's another aspect of planer design that varies widely. Some models have single-edged knives that allow for resharpening. Others have double-edged, disposable knives that you reverse when one edge becomes dull and you throw away when both do. Various systems are employed for housing the knives in the cutterhead, including lock-down screws and springs. If your model doesn't come with a knife-adjusting jig, you'll want to get one when you replace the blades. And while you're at it, purchase a second set of blades so you can keep working when one set becomes dull or gets nicked.

■ **DUST HOOD:** This feature is not standard on most models and can be purchased separately. It is a worthwhile accessory. Benchtop planers produce an astonishing amount of shavings in just a few passes. A dust hood hooked to a dust-collection system will keep shavings from piling up into a safety hazard and save you hours of cleanup time.

■ **MOLDING CUTTERS:** Molding knives are a feature of larger molder-planer machines. Interchangeable knives will form molding patterns to turn flat boards into decorative moldings. Machines with this increased versatility cost more than a benchtop planer and are considerably larger. Molding profiles can be made with other tools.

PLANER SAFETY

With its cutterhead and knives enclosed in the housing of the tool, the thickness planer is one of the safest shop tools to operate. Like all tools powered by universal motors, however, benchtop planers are noisy. Even stationary planers make quite a racket when their knives are shearing off wood. Ear protection is a must with these machines, as is eye protection. In addition, observe the following practices:

■ Though kickback is unlikely, stand to one side of a planer, not behind it.

■ In the unlikely event the workpiece jams, don't attempt to pull it or push it out. Turn off the power and raise the cutterhead.

■ Never put your hands in a running machine and always unplug the planer before making adjustments.

TROUBLESHOOTING YOUR WORK

If your planer isn't producing absolutely smooth surfaces, there is usually a remedy to be found. Here are a few common ones.

■ To minimize end snipe, try making shallower cuts and keeping the stock flat throughout its entire pass. Support the end of long stock with outfeed rollers. Or, plan for snipe by planing longer stock, then cutting the sniped ends off.

■ A wavy surface indicates one knife is set higher than the other. Unplug the machine and reset the knives.

■ Thin raised lines of uncut wood mean the knives are chipped. For a quick fix, loosen one knife and move it about $1/32$ inch to one side or the other. That way one knife will take out the line left by the other. Reset the knife and tighten it. Sharpen or replace the knives as soon as possible.

COSTS

Benchtop planers list for around $400. Most of the models with the features described above can be purchased for $300–$400.

USING A BENCHTOP PLANER

Although assembly and setup of a planer will vary from model to model, the following rules of thumb apply to all models.

■ Especially in rough stock, check for nails, staples, bits of wire, and anything left over from a salvage process that could nick the blade. Use a metal detector if you have any doubt, especially in rough stock like barn lumber. It's common for the head of a fastener to have rusted off, leaving the rest of it lurking under the surface. Find it before your planer does.

■ Set the workpiece in the planer and lower the cutterhead until it just contacts the work. Take the stock off the table and set the cutting depth at $\frac{1}{16}$ inch for pine and other softwoods, $\frac{1}{32}$ inch for hardwoods.

■ Turn the power on and feed the workpiece into the planer until the infeed rollers take over. Let the stock come to rest on the outfeed table or extensions. Pulling the stock through the planer can cause miscuts.

■ Repeat the above procedure until the board is planed smooth to the proper thickness; use a shallow cutting depth for the final pass.

■ Planers won't take cupping and warping out of a board—the rollers will simply compress the distortion flat, and it will spring back on the outfeed side. Use a jointer to remove warping, followed by a pass through your table saw (see illustration on page 77).

■ Planers will handle thin stock and short pieces without trouble if you use the techniques illustrated at right.

PLANING LONG AND SHORT STOCK

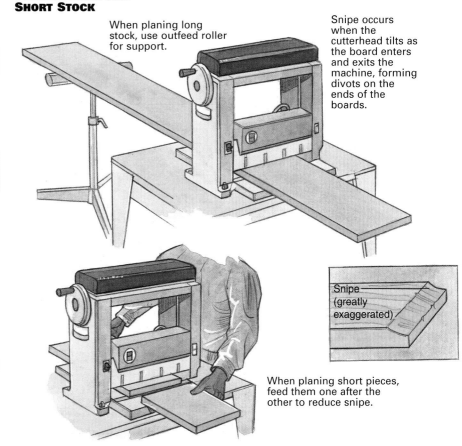

When planing long stock, use outfeed roller for support.

Snipe occurs when the cutterhead tilts as the board enters and exits the machine, forming divots on the ends of the boards.

Snipe (greatly exaggerated)

When planing short pieces, feed them one after the other to reduce snipe.

PLANING BEVELS

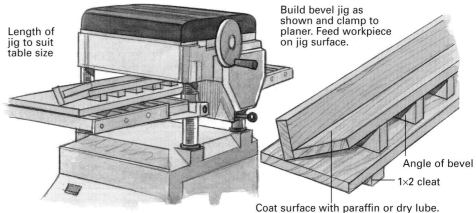

Length of jig to suit table size

Build bevel jig as shown and clamp to planer. Feed workpiece on jig surface.

Angle of bevel

1×2 cleat

Coat surface with paraffin or dry lube.

PLANING THIN STOCK

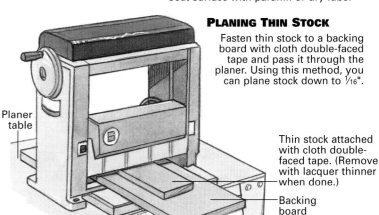

Fasten thin stock to a backing board with cloth double-faced tape and pass it through the planer. Using this method, you can plane stock down to $\frac{1}{16}$".

Planer table

Thin stock attached with cloth double-faced tape. (Remove with lacquer thinner when done.)

Backing board

SANDERS

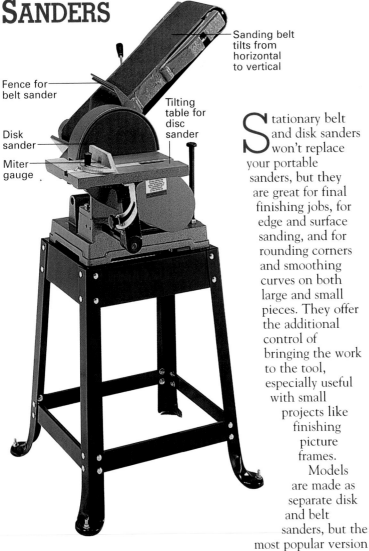

Fence for belt sander

Disk sander

Miter gauge

Sanding belt tilts from horizontal to vertical

Tilting table for disc sander

Stationary belt and disk sanders won't replace your portable sanders, but they are great for final finishing jobs, for edge and surface sanding, and for rounding corners and smoothing curves on both large and small pieces. They offer the additional control of bringing the work to the tool, especially useful with small projects like finishing picture frames.

Models are made as separate disk and belt sanders, but the most popular version found in workshops is the combination sander. You get the best of both tools run by one motor, and often at a savings over the price of separate tools. If you're looking at a sander that doesn't come with a stand and you're not going to mount the sander on a worktable, be sure to factor in the cost of a stand, from $70 to more than $150.

A STATIONARY SANDER CAN...

■ Rapidly sand angles, bevels, chamfers, and straight edges smooth
■ Precisely adjust miter cuts and compound angles
■ Sand joints flush
■ Flatten small faces
■ Smooth and true large and small pieces
■ Sand outside (and on some machines, inside) curves

SIZES

Combination sanders come in both benchtop and floor-standing models. At the small end of the scale are models with 1-inch belts and small disks. They're useful for sharpening and small sanding jobs, but not built for work with larger stock.

After these small units, there's not much variation in belt widths between the benchtop and floor

models. Although at least one midsize benchtop model comes with a 4-inch belt, machines for home workshops will typically feature a 6×48-inch belt. The wider and longer the belt, the more working surface you have and the longer the belt will last.

Disk diameter varies considerably between benchtop and floor models. Benchtop sanding disks run from 5 to 12 inches in diameter. In floor models, you'll see a lot of 9-inch disks, some 12-inch disks, and a few at 16 inches. An 8- or 9-inch disk should be able to handle most of your work.

TABLES

Benchtop models have two tables and though a few are made of cast aluminum to reduce weight, a surprising number of benchtop styles use cast iron, a definite plus.

More floor models are made than benchtop tools, with about an equal number of 1- and 2-table models, most made of cast iron. A single table that you can reposition from disk to belt use and vice versa may help hold costs down, but increases setup time slightly, a factor that may affect your costs if you have "production-line" projects in your plans.

Some tables are slotted for miter-gauge use; others are not. If a miter-gauge slot won't push you over budget, buy a model with one. You can't freehand your approach to a disk or belt with any accuracy. You can, however, overcome the absence of a miter gauge with guides clamped to the table.

Regardless of how many tables a unit has, they should tilt at least at 45 degrees for bevel sanding. And the belt should lock both vertically and horizontally. Look for easy setup and positive table locks.

POWER

Power starts out at ⅓ hp for smaller disks and rises incrementally with disk size. For an 8- or 9-inch disk, ½ to ¾ hp should be sufficient; for a 12-inch model, 1½ hp. Belt speeds start at around 1,500 feet per minute and disks rotate between 1,700 and 3,400 rpm. Speeds at the bottom of the range will give you slightly more control over the work, but they may not remove material as fast as you'd like. Speeds of 1,800 to 2,500 rpm are a good compromise.

Make sure your sanding disk is square to the table by holding a square against the disk and the table (remove the sandpaper first). Adjust the position of the table until the square is flush against both surfaces.

To mount a new belt, release the tension and lower the upper drum. Remove the old belt and slide the new one over the drums with the arrow pointing down. Raise the upper drum, center the belt, and tighten the tension to remove slack. Turn the sander on and off quickly and adjust the tracking so the belt does not slip off.

OSCILLATING-SPINDLE AND THICKNESS SANDERS

Oscillating-spindle and thickness sanders are becoming more popular in the home-workshop market.

An oscillating-spindle sander might remind you of a shaper—it has a spindle in the center of a table, and it is used to shape and smooth surfaces. Instead of shaper heads, sanding sleeves of different diameters and grits are mounted on the 4- to 4½-inch spindle, which rotates at about 200 rpm and oscillates up and down at about 60 strokes per minute. They're not as common as other shop sanders, so you may have to look a little harder to find one. When you do, you can expect to pay at least $200. Prices increase from there to more than $1,500. Look for a large, flat table and easy-to-change sanding sleeves.

Thickness sanders (or open-end drum sanders) are large machines with heavy-duty motors designed to do delicate work—uniformly sanding large sheets or panels to within .010 inch. Their drums, housed in an adjustable head, are wrapped with abrasive strips, and the work is fed through the machine by a conveyor system at variable speeds up to 15 feet per minute. Capacities will vary with the price, as will sanding tolerances. Sanding a 32-inch width (in two passes on a 16-inch machine) is well within the reach of most models. Some thickness sanders are mounted on a stand and others come without a stand, so you need to figure the extra cost for them. Expect prices to run in the $750 to $850 range, higher for commercial machines.

OSCILLATING-SPINDLE SANDER

Spindle moves up and down as it rotates

THICKNESS SANDER

Horizontal sanding drum (inside)

Belt carries work through sander.

SANDERS
continued

■ **BELT CHANGING AND TRACKING:**
Manufacturers have come up with a number
of ways to speed belt changing and tracking.
Some models have quick-release belt-
changing mechanisms and toolless tracking
adjustments. Thumbscrew tracking is
especially quick. These features add a great
deal of convenience to your use of the sander.

■ **DUST PORTS:** Power sanders send a lot
of dust into the air and on the floor, and
almost all current models have a dust port
suitable for hook-up to your dust-collection
system.

SANDING EDGES WITH A STATIONARY BELT SANDER

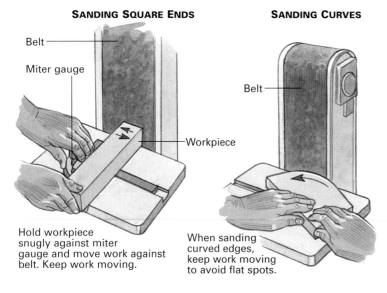

SANDING SQUARE ENDS

Belt

Miter gauge

Workpiece

Hold workpiece
snugly against miter
gauge and move work against
belt. Keep work moving.

SANDING CURVES

Belt

When sanding
curved edges,
keep work moving
to avoid flat spots.

SANDING MITERS, BEVELS, AND CHAMFERS

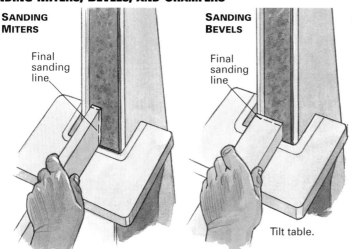

SANDING MITERS

Final
sanding
line

SANDING BEVELS

Final
sanding
line

Tilt table.

CHAMFERING

Prices of small benchtop models may surprise
you. Units start at less than $100 and increase
to as much as $1,000, although discount and
volume-sales distributors may be able to
knock $150 off the high-end price. Good
light-duty sanders go for about $150, but
heavier 1-hp models will run $400 to $500.

A good floor model sander with a 9-inch
disk will run about $200 to $250. Better
models with convenience features cost
between $250 and $450.

Because the belt moves in one direction only,
it is more suited to with-the-grain sanding.
Cross-grain sanding is fine also, but removes
wood about twice as fast as in-line work. In
general, you should sand surfaces with the
table locked horizontally.

■ Because the action of the belt tends to pull
the work with it, always grip the work firmly
and stand to the side of the table, not along
the line where a piece could be ejected. Use
the manufacturer's stop block or one of your
own design. (See the illustration on the
opposite page.) Move the work from side to
side to equalize belt wear.

■ To sand contours, remove the top guard
and with the sander mounted horizontally,
apply the work with gentle pressure to the
curve of the top drum. You'll do most
contour-sanding freehand. Keep the work
moving along the contour to avoid flat spots,
and work across the entire width of the belt.

■ Edge sanding is best done with the belt in
the vertical position (or angled) or with the
table tilted. If the edge moves from a straight
to a curved shape, start on the straight side
and sand into the curve. Keep the work
moving. For square ends, angles, and bevels,
move the work
directly forward
and across the
belt. Use a miter
gauge or
clamped guides
whenever
possible.

To sand angled,
beveled, and
chamfered edges,
tilt the sander table
to the correct angle,
and sand back to
the mark.

USING A FENCE

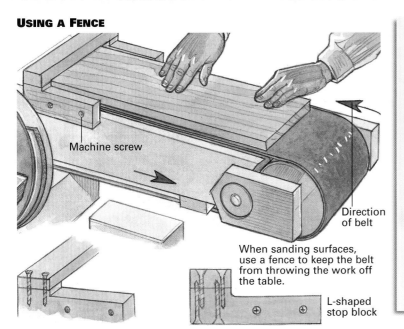

Machine screw

Direction of belt

When sanding surfaces, use a fence to keep the belt from throwing the work off the table.

L-shaped stop block

SANDER SAFETY

Abrasives have cutting edges, and coarse abrasives can cut quickly. Keeping your fingers away from the surfaces is a must, but so is anticipating which way the tool will eject the workpiece if it slips. Observe these safety practices:
- Wear eye and ear protection and a mask or respirator.
- Use a jig for small work or clamp it to a larger piece.
- Always sand to the down side of the belt or disk.
- Keep loose clothing away from moving parts. A stationary sander can pull you into the machine before you can shut it off.

SANDING INSIDE CURVES

Use the drum at the top of the belt sander to shape curved surfaces.

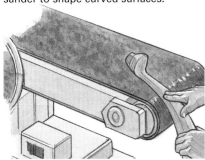

ROUNDING AN EDGE

Rotate workpiece until you get the desired shape.

When using the disk sander, keep the work on the down side of the abrasive. Use light pressure.

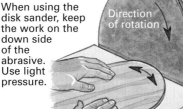

Direction of rotation

SANDING ANGLES

Use a miter gauge when sanding angles. Keep the work on the down side of disk rotation.

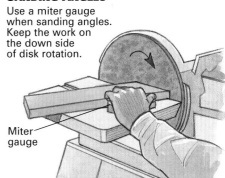

Miter gauge

DISK SANDING

Many disk sanders use pressure-sensitive adhesive to adhere the paper to the disk. To make sure new paper stays in place, clamp it to the disk for a day before using it. To remove the paper without tearing, warm it with a hair dryer first.
- Disks don't always sand with the grain because they rotate.
- Different points on the disk move at different surface speeds. At the center, the speed approaches zero feet per minute, then increases as you move toward the edge. Use this to your advantage with delicate work.
- Always sand with the work on the down side of the disk. This presses the work onto the table and gives you greater control.
- Keep the work moving, especially on curves. Use sweeping motions to round off curves; stopping creates flat spots.
- Power sanders work best when you don't rush or use heavy pressure. Too much pressure clogs the paper quickly and can cause burn spots on the surface of the work.

SANDING CHAMFERS AND CIRCLES

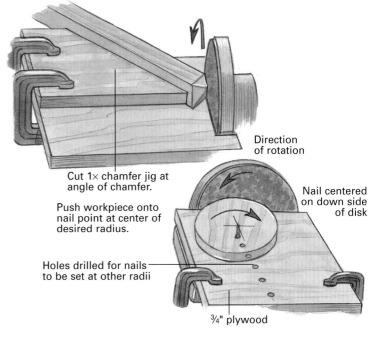

Cut 1× chamfer jig at angle of chamfer.

Push workpiece onto nail point at center of desired radius.

Holes drilled for nails to be set at other radii

Direction of rotation

Nail centered on down side of disk

¾" plywood

LATHE

A LATHE CAN...

■ Turn table legs, spindles, candlesticks, and other decorative objects
■ Create bowls, platters, and other vessels

The transition from general home maintenance projects to more serious woodworking is a natural one. It often takes place over several years. For many, wood turning—making bowls, pens, and decorative objects on a lathe—becomes an abiding interest, even a passion. Others like to make

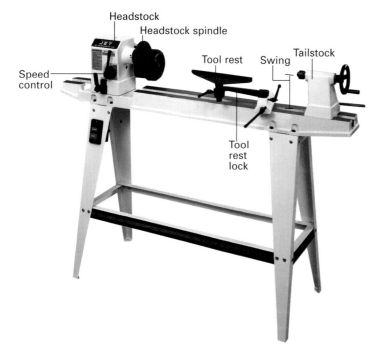

Headstock
Headstock spindle
Tool rest   Swing   Tailstock
Speed control
Tool rest lock

fine furniture, often with turned wood legs and other parts. Either case requires a lathe. The question is, of course, which one?

There are more than 100 different lathe models on the market. There are minilathes, midi-lathes (actually midsize benchtop models), benchtop lathes, floor models (often with the same capacities as their benchtop brothers), duplicators, and bowl turners. Between the categories, there's a lot of overlap, with manufacturers and distributors using the same terms with different meanings; one person's minilathe may be the next person's benchtop.

SORTING THINGS OUT

To cut through the confusion, make a list of the kinds of objects you want to produce. If you're never going to make things larger than pens or candlesticks—and if your space is limited—then you need a minilathe. For turning longer objects, such as chair and table legs, a larger benchtop lathe or a floor model is in order. These larger lathes will make smaller things with just as much precision. If bowl turning is your only love, look for a large benchtop or standard-size floor model with a swivel headstock or a single-purpose bowl-turning lathe. One of the benchtop or floor models will offer the most versatility for general wood turning.

WHAT TO LOOK FOR

■ **CAPACITY:** Lathe capacity is determined by the largest diameter and length of stock it can turn. The *swing* of a lathe is the distance from the bed to the center of the spindle—half the diameter the lathe can turn. The distance between the headstock and tailstock determines length. A lathe with 5- or 6-inch swing and 14-inch length is adequate for small projects. For table legs, you'll need at least a 36-inch turning length.

■ **POWER:** Power generally follows size. Smaller lathes start out at ⅙ hp and top out at 1½ hp. A ½- to ¾-hp motor should be about right. Stepping up to a larger lathe, a 12×36, for example, you'll need power in the ¾- to 1-hp range. Turning large, heavy bowls will demand a tough tool—a minimum of 1½ hp.

■ **SPEED RANGE:** Speed range and control are important. Roughing large stock requires slow speeds, 500 rpm or less. Finishing is high-speed work. For all-around general-purpose turning, look for a range between about 600 and 3,000 rpm. Some models offer continuous electronic speed control, and others have a mechanical speed changer that varies the size of split pulleys. The continuous speed controls are not a necessity, but they are far more convenient than switching belts on cone pulleys.

■ **STABILITY:** Vibration is the chief enemy of fine wood turning. Beds are made so the tailstock slides in a cast-iron, aluminum, or steel frame or on tubular steel rods. Cast iron tends to be more stable than tubular steel.

ALIGNING LATHE CENTERS

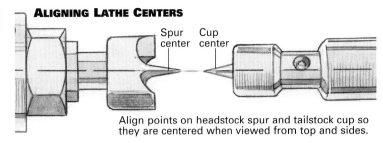

Spur center Cup center

Align points on headstock spur and tailstock cup so they are centered when viewed from top and sides.

LOADING STOCK IN A LATHE

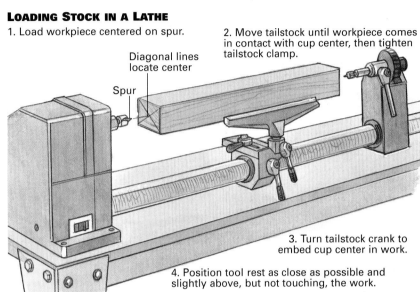

1. Load workpiece centered on spur.

Diagonal lines locate center

Spur

2. Move tailstock until workpiece comes in contact with cup center, then tighten tailstock clamp.

3. Turn tailstock crank to embed cup center in work.

4. Position tool rest as close as possible and slightly above, but not touching, the work.

LATHE SPEEDS

Most lathe instruction manuals list speed guidelines for stock of different diameters, usually given as the spindle speed in rpm. When you start with square or other unround stock, make your first roughing cuts at a slow speed. When the stock is rounded and in balance, increase to the suggested speed for shaping and finishing.

Speed at the workpiece surface—the rate at which the material moves past the tool's cutting edge—is most important. Larger-diameter stock will have a faster surface speed (measured in feet per minute—fpm) than smaller stock at the same lathe spindle speed (rpm).

The correct speed also varies with the hardness of the stock and the type of turning tool you are using. When in doubt about lathe speed for any operation, start with a lower speed. You can then slowly increase the speed for optimum cutting.

A tilt-down panel attached to the open legs of this lathe stand holds the accessories and tools.

LATHE
continued

LAYING OUT THE WORK

1. Visualize and sketch the profile of your work.

2. Cut sketch on centerline and transfer to cardboard or hardboard to make a template. Extend lines of profile to opposite edge of template to make a marking gauge.

3. Transfer profile lines to workpiece. Then, with lathe rotating slowly, extend lines around surface.

4. Use template to check your work.

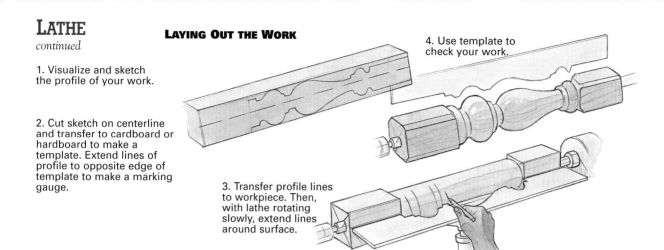

USING A GOUGE

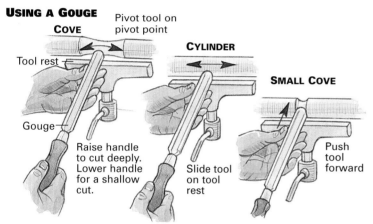

COVE — Pivot tool on pivot point

Tool rest

Gouge

Raise handle to cut deeply. Lower handle for a shallow cut.

CYLINDER

Slide tool on tool rest

SMALL COVE

Push tool forward

USING A SKEW

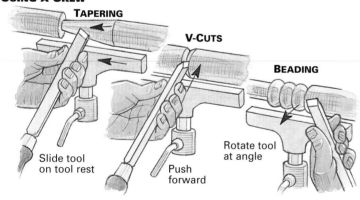

TAPERING

Slide tool on tool rest

V-CUTS

Push forward

BEADING

Rotate tool at angle

USING A ROUNDNOSE

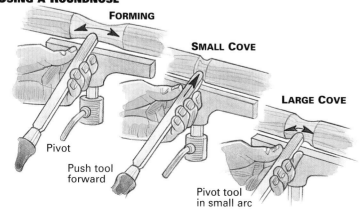

FORMING

Pivot

Push tool forward

SMALL COVE

LARGE COVE

Pivot tool in small arc

Stability is also a function of headstock and tailstock weight—the heavier the better. And for increased versatility, get a unit with a headstock that swivels. Locking the headstock at a right angle to the bed allows you to turn bowls larger than the swing.

■ **SPINDLE:** Headstock spindle sizes are designated by diameter and threading. The three most common are 1 inch (diameter) × 8 threads per inch (tpi), ¾ inch × 16 tpi, and 1¼ inches × 8 tpi. If you plan to do large turnings, consider a lathe with a large spindle. A tailstock with a live center that rotates with the work is handy.

■ **TOOL REST:** Tool rests come in a wide variety of sizes, shapes, and lengths. What's important is that the rest slides easily on the table, adjusts quickly to the right height, and locks securely.

COSTS

Not all minilathes and benchtop models come with miniprices—some list well above $1,000. Some models with 6-inch swings list for $200 to $250, with the more versatile models at $400 to $500. A high-quality 12×36-inch lathe will cost $600 or more.

START WITH THE RIGHT STOCK

Your success with wood turning will depend not only on the quality of your lathe and the level of your skills, but also on the quality of the raw stock. You can't just chuck in any old piece of wood and get good results. Stock that is split or checked (cracked across the grain) will catch the tool and splinter or break. Knots will make the tool jump off the work and may pop out, leaving holes.

Buy commercial wood turning blanks or make your own—only from "select or better" lumber. You'll like the variety you can achieve with your own blanks, fashioned in your table saw and jointer. Alternate colors to get dramatic effects, but keep the grain of the joined pieces in the same direction to reduce cross-grain splintering. Your final shape should be square, with chamfered edges to speed the initial rounding.

USING A LATHE

■ **LAYOUT:** Visualize the final shape of the piece and sketch it on paper until it conforms exactly to the shape you want. Then transfer the design to a stiff cardboard template and cut it exactly down the center. Draw lines from the profile edge to the straight edge of the template at each point where the contours change. Cut out the profile side.

■ **MOUNT THE BLANK:** Find the center of the blank by drawing lines across the diagonals at both ends and push the center point against the headstock spur. Move the tailstock so its point pierces the center of the blank at the other end and locks the tailstock. Tighten the tailstock crank until you can't move the blank.

■ **TOOL REST:** Adjust the tool rest so that it's about ⅛ inch from the edge of the blank and ⅛ inch higher than the centerline of the workpiece.

■ **SELECT THE SPEED** that's appropriate to the cutter and the size of the blank—slow speeds for roughing and large stock, higher speeds for smaller stock and finishing.

■ **ONCE YOU'VE COMPLETED THE INITIAL ROUNDING,** transfer your profile marks to the blank with a pencil, and with the work turning, mark its circumference.

LATHE SAFETY

Lathes are relatively safe. Any tool with moving parts, however, poses potential risks. Always take the following precautions:
■ Wear safety glasses or goggles and avoid loose clothing or jewelry that could get caught in the machine or the workpiece.
■ Make sure workpiece is centered and secure between the headstock and tailstock.
■ Use speeds that are appropriate to the material, tool, and kind of cut. Shallow cuts are easier and reduce the chance of the cutting tool catching in the work.
■ Avoid using stock that is damaged or contains checks, cracks, or splits.
■ Always lay the turning tool firmly against the tool rest before advancing the cutting edge into the workpiece.

■ **AS YOU TURN THE PROFILES,** use the cut-out edge of the template to check your work. The illustrations show basic cuts with some turning tools. Hands-on instruction from an experienced wood turner will pay off in increased confidence and competence.

USING A PARTING TOOL

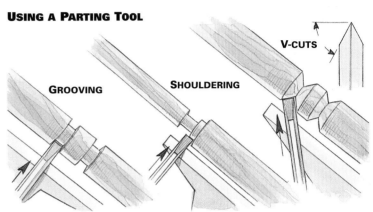

V-CUTS

GROOVING   SHOULDERING

Start with handle slightly below tool rest and raise it as tool begins to cut.

USING A SQUARENOSE

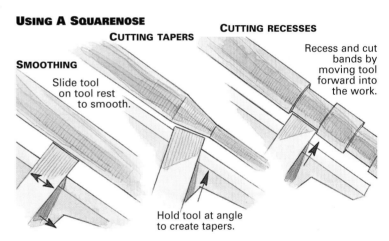

CUTTING TAPERS   CUTTING RECESSES

SMOOTHING

Slide tool on tool rest to smooth.

Recess and cut bands by moving tool forward into the work.

Hold tool at angle to create tapers.

TURNING ON A FACEPLATE

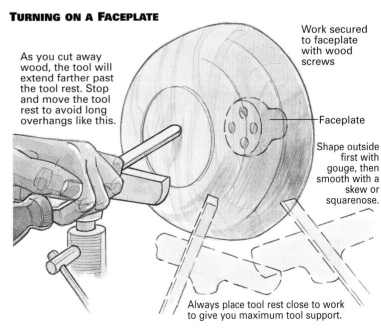

As you cut away wood, the tool will extend farther past the tool rest. Stop and move the tool rest to avoid long overhangs like this.

Work secured to faceplate with wood screws

Faceplate

Shape outside first with gouge, then smooth with a skew or squarenose.

Always place tool rest close to work to give you maximum tool support.

MULTIPURPOSE MACHINE

American multipurpose machines (right and below) pack five or more tools into the space of a lathe.

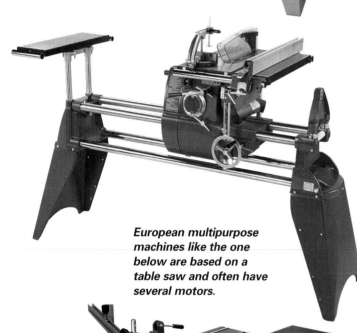

European multipurpose machines like the one below are based on a table saw and often have several motors.

With one to three motors and a number of different tools—all contained within the space of a worktable or less—multipurpose machines can be a woodworker's dream, especially for those who have limited shop space but need—or want—the functions of several tools. Multitool machines (sometimes called combination tools) are common in European shops and another style has been popular with many American tool buyers for 50 years.

American machines (shown at left), which generally look like a lathe, offer at least five basic woodworking tools: table saw, lathe, drill press, disc sander, and horizontal boring machine. A power take-off allows the addition of other tools, such as a band saw and a jointer, and many accessories are available to expand the range of uses. One American-made model boasts 10 functions, including three metalworking tools.

European combination machines house several tools in one cabinet. The tools share a table and sliding table, but usually have separate motors. The five-tool model shown at left has three 3-hp motors to power a table saw, thickness planer, jointer, shaper, and mortising machine.

DO YOU NEED A MULTIPURPOSE MACHINE?

The answer to this question is a double-edged sword. On the one hand, you can ask yourself whether you'll ever need a horizontal boring machine. On the other, even though one of these models may include a tool you don't have much use for, its price may well be less than the combined prices of separate tools of the same

Most multipurpose machines feature a table saw function. On the American machines, the saw table tilts rather than the blade, which can limit the length of stock you can bevel cut.

You can change quickly from one function to another with this European machine. The five tools rival individual tools in power and work capacity, but take up much less workshop space.

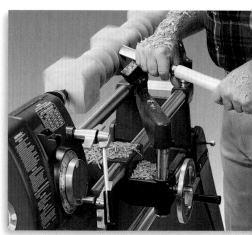

Make sure capabilities and working capacities of a multipurpose machine match or exceed your needs. If you want to turn large pieces, such as this baluster, look at the American machines.

quality. American-made models start at about $2,000 and go up to around $3,200. The combined costs of a quality table saw, lathe, and drill press alone can add up to more than that. The two-tool European counterparts start at about $6,000, with five-tool units running from $8,000 to almost $11,000. Although these prices might exceed the combined prices of separate tools, the European models are compact, robustly built, and claim precise machining tolerances and adjustments. Their cast-iron tables account for a good deal of their weight—from 1,100 to 1,600 pounds.

PROS AND CONS

One oft-cited drawback of multipurpose machines is that they don't let you build up your shop with a carefully chosen selection of tools. You get all the tools at once. If you dislike the way one works, you'll have to either figure out how to work around the problem or buy a single-purpose tool—which defeats the purpose for buying a multipurpose tool in the first place.

The need to change the setup of multipurpose machines to perform different tasks is also cited as a drawback. In fact, users usually don't find this a problem once they start working with the machines. One European manufacturer claims it takes only 20 seconds to change from one tool to another—a speed due in part to design and in part to its three motors. Changeover will usually take longer on American models. You can minimize some of the time loss by organizing your project so you can group operations, such as sawing, to reduce the number of times you need to change. Besides,

as many woodworkers point out, you don't use more than one tool at a time, anyway.

BUYING A MULTIPURPOSE MACHINE

More than any other tool purchase, buying a multipurpose machine requires careful research. Get all the information you can, especially from reviews in woodworking publications and Internet users' forums. When you find a feature that's getting poor marks from users, consider how important it is to you and whether you might be able to work around the problem. Make sure the machine will do the jobs you want it to. Ask someone who owns one if you can try it out, or watch for live demonstrations at fairs or woodworking shows. Contact dealers or manufacturers; they will gladly furnish catalogs, specifications, and information.

With the head pivoted up, an American machine becomes a drill press. Relatively large capacity, continuously variable speeds, and a tilting table make it versatile.

BENCH GRINDER

A bench grinder is not technically a woodworking tool, but it's an important part of any shop. It makes quick work of keeping the edges of chisels, planer and jointer blades, and other cutting tools sharp.

Although single-wheel grinders are available, the most common model for home shops has two wheels—one coarse-grit (or medium-grit) and one fine-grit—mounted on either end of the motor. The size of the grinder is determined by the size of the wheel, ranging from 5 to 10 inches. A 6-inch grinder is standard for a home workshop. You'll find many units of this size on the market, most powered by a 1/3-hp motor—plenty for normal

use. Face guards, spark deflectors, and tool rests on both wheels are usually standard equipment. Work lights are standard on some machines, and are worth the price as an accessory on grinders not so equipped.

The tops of the wheels rotate toward you, which allows you to hold cutting edges on the edge of the wheel against the rotation. Before you start sharpening, adjust the tool rest so it's about 1/8 inch away from the edge of the wheel and set it to the angle for the tool you're sharpening. The original factory angle of the edge is almost always the proper angle for the tool.

Holding the tool on the tool rest, move the tool lightly across the edge of the wheel. Check the angle and readjust the tool rest, if necessary. Then make light passes again and check the edge carefully. Dip the tool edge in water frequently to cool it—don't let it turn blue. Many grinders have a built-in water trough for cooling. Finish the edge by honing it on a whetstone.

DRESSING THE WHEEL

A grinding wheel constantly renews its surface during use. Dull grains fly off, exposing fresh grains. Keep the wheel surface square by frequently dressing it. When the grinder reaches full speed, press the wheel dresser against the edge of the wheel and move it side to side. Support the dresser on the tool rest and keep it parallel to the wheel.

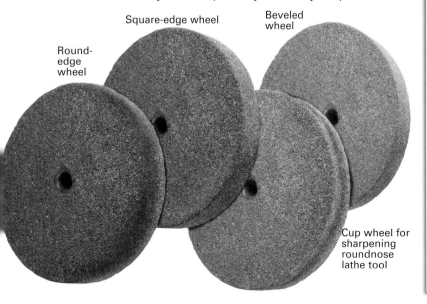

Round-edge wheel

Square-edge wheel

Beveled wheel

Cup wheel for sharpening roundnose lathe tool

A low-speed wet-wheel grinder is ideal for sharpening chisels, plane irons, and other fine edges.

This grinder combines a low-speed wet wheel with a high-speed dry wheel for general use.

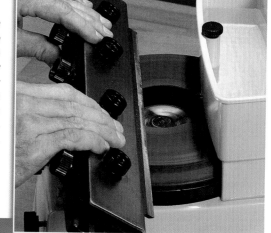

An adjustable accessory tool rest is a good addition to most bench grinders. A rigid, accurate rest is crucial to precise sharpening.

A slow-speed wet-wheel grinder is often considered the best piece of equipment for sharpening knives, chisels, plane irons, and other tempered tools. The slow-turning wheel (it usually goes 400 rpm or less) runs in a water bath, which both cools the stone and keeps it clear of grinding particles. Water carried by the stone helps cool the tool being sharpened too. Unlike a high-speed grinder, this one won't heat the tool edge to blue heat, which takes away its temper. The stone is usually a finer grit than on a dry-wheel grinder, but the water helps it grind faster than a dry stone of the same grit. The wet-wheel grinder can produce a sharper edge than a dry grinder.

Wet-wheel grinders are available with a vertical wheel (shown top left) or a horizontal one (above right). Combination grinders, like the one shown in the photo at center left, have both a slow wet wheel and a higher-speed dry wheel. On these, the dry wheel spins at about the same speed as on a standard bench grinder.

A precision sliding guide makes it easy to sharpen jointer knives and other wide edges accurately on a horizontal low-speed, wet-wheel grinder.

BENCH-GRINDER SAFETY

Always observe the following safety practices when using a bench grinder.
■ Wear eye, ear, and face protection.
■ Use a fixed tempered glass screen guard when using the grinder.
■ Keep tool rests properly adjusted.
■ Stand to one side until the wheel reaches full speed. And if you accidentally drop a wheel before mounting it, throw it away. It may fly apart when the grinder comes to speed.

Exchange the grinding wheel for a buffing wheel and run rouge polishing compound on its surface to polish metals.

MANUFACTURERS, DISTRIBUTORS, AND DEALERS

ACCUSET
888/222-8144
www.accuset.com

AMAZON.COM
www.amazon.com

BELSAW
800/468-4449
www.belsaw.com

BEST TOOL SITES.COM
www.besttoolsites.com

BLACK & DECKER
800/544-6986
www.blackanddecker.com

BOSCH
877/267-2499
www.boschtools.com

CRAFTSMAN—SEARS
800/377-7414
www.sears.com/craftsman

DELTA MACHINERY
800/438-2486
www.deltawoodworking.com

DEWALT
800/433-9258
www.dewalt.com

DREMEL
800/437-3635
www.dremel.com

DUO-FAST
888/386-3278
www.duo-fast.com

EXCALIBUR SOMMERVILLE GROUP
800/357-4118
www.toolsplus.com/
toolsplus/exc.html

FEIN POWER TOOLS
800/441-9878
www.feinus.com

FESTOOL
888/463-3786
www.festool-usa.com

FREUD USA
800/334-4107
www.freudtools.com

GENERAL INTERNATIONAL
819/472-1161
www.general.ca

GENERAL TOOL & SUPPLY
800/783-3411
www. generaltool.com

GRIZZLY INDUSTRIAL
800/523-4777
www.grizzly.com

HEGNER
800/727-6553
www.advmachinery.com/hegner

HIGHLAND HARDWARE
888/500-4466
www.highland-hardware.com/

HITACHI POWER TOOLS
800/706-7337
www.hitachi.com

INCA
800/221-2942
www.garrettwade.com

INGERSOLL RAND— ARO TOOLS
www.ingersoll-rand.com

JET EQUIPMENT & TOOLS
800/274-6848
www.jettools.com

LAGUNA TOOLS
800/234-1976
www.lagunatools.com

LAMELLO COLONIAL SAW
800/252-6355
www.csaw.com

LOBO MACHINE POWER TOOLS
800/786-5626
www.lobomachine.com

MAKITA
800/462-5482
www.makita.com

METABO
800/638-2264
www.metabousa.com

MILLER INDUSTRIAL SUPPLY
800/230-7999
www.millerindsupply.com

MILWAUKEE ELECTRIC TOOL
800/414-6527
www.mil-electric-tool.com

MURPHY-RODGERS—DUST COLLECTION SYSTEMS
323/587-4118
www.murphy-rodgers.com

ONEWAY MANUFACTURING
800/565-7288
www.oneway.on.ca

PANASONIC POWER TOOLS
800/338-0552
www.panasonic.com

PENN STATE INDUSTRIES
800/377-7297
www.pennstateind.com

PORTER-CABLE
800/487-8665
www.porter-cable.com

POWERMATIC
800/248-0144
www.powermatic.com

RBI INDUSTRIES
800/487-2623
www.rbiwoodtools.com

RIDGID
800/474-3443
www.ridgidwoodworking.com

RIGHT-TOOL.COM
978/562-8555 (fax)
www.right-tool.com

ROBLAND— LAGUNA TOOLS
800/234-1976
www.lagunatools.com

RYOBI POWER TOOLS
800/323-4615
www.ryobi.com

SECO MACHINERY
888/558-4628
www.seco-usa.com

7 CORNERS HARDWARE
800/328-0457
www.7corners.com

SHOPSMITH INC
800/543-7586
www.shopsmith.com

SIOUX TOOLS
800/722-7290
www.siouxtools.com

SKIL
877/754-5999 (SKIL 999)
www.skiltools.com

SMITHY TOOLS
800/476-4849
www.smithy.com

STANLEY BOSTITCH
800/556-6696
http://www.Stan1eyworks.com

STAR TOOLS
888/678-8777
www.411web.com/s/startools

SUNHILL MACHINERY
800/929-4321
www.sunhillnic.com

TOOLS PLUS
800/222-6133
www.toolsplus.com

TRADESMAN POWERTOOLS
800/243-5114
www.tradesman-rexon.com

CRAFT SUPPLIES USA WOOD TURNING
800/551-8876
www.woodturnerscatalog.com

VIRUTEX
800/868-9663
www.virutex.com

WILKE MACHINERY
800/235-2100
www.wilkemach.com

WOODCRAFT
800/225-1153
www.woodcraft.com

WOODCRAFTER'S SUPPLY
412/367-4330
www.woodcrafterssupply.com

WOODWORKER'S DEPOT
800/891-9003
www.woodworkersdepot.com

WOODWORKER'S SUPPLY
800/645-9292
www.woodworker.com

WOODWORKERS WAREHOUSE
800/877-7899
www.woodworkerswarehouse.com

INDEX

METRIC CONVERSIONS

U.S. Units to Metric Equivalents			Metric Units to U.S. Equivalents		
To Convert From	Multiply By	To Get	To Convert From	Multiply By	To Get
Inches	25.4	Millimeters	Millimeters	0.0394	Inches
Inches	2.54	Centimeters	Centimeters	0.3937	Inches
Feet	30.48	Centimeters	Centimeters	0.0328	Feet
Feet	0.3048	Meters	Meters	3.2808	Feet
Yards	0.9144	Meters	Meters	1.0936	Yards
Square inches	6.4516	Square centimeters	Square centimeters	0.1550	Square inches
Square feet	0.0929	Square meters	Square meters	10.764	Square feet
Square yards	0.8361	Square meters	Square meters	1.1960	Square yards
Acres	0.4047	Hectares	Hectares	2.4711	Acres
Cubic inches	16.387	Cubic centimeters	Cubic centimeters	0.0610	Cubic inches
Cubic feet	0.0283	Cubic meters	Cubic meters	35.315	Cubic feet
Cubic feet	28.316	Liters	Liters	0.0353	Cubic feet
Cubic yards	0.7646	Cubic meters	Cubic meters	1.308	Cubic yards
Cubic yards	764.55	Liters	Liters	0.0013	Cubic yards

To convert from degrees Fahrenheit (F) to degrees Celsius (C), first subtract 32, then multiply by ⁵⁄₉.

To convert from degrees Celsius to degrees Fahrenheit, multiply by ⁹⁄₅, then add 32.